Freire's Key Terms

FREIRE IN FOCUS

Series editors: Greg William Misiaszek and Carlos Alberto Torres

This series of short-format books provide readers a diverse range of Paulo Freire's work and Freireans' reinventions towards social justice both inside and outside education, without readers needing any prior knowledge of his scholarship. The books offer new perspectives on the work of Freire's teaching, ideas, methods and philosophies. Each book will introduce Freire's work so it is easily understood by a wider audience without overly simplifying the depth of his scholarship.

Advisory Board
Ali Abdi; Marina Aparicio Barberán; Pep Aparicio Guadas; Michael Apple; Rima Apple; Ângela Antunes; N'Dri T. Assié-Lumumba; Oscar Azmitia Barranco; Lesley Bartlett; Kumari Beck; Tina Besley; ChenWei Chang; Luiza Cortesão; Regina Cortina; José Cossa; Sonia Couto; Eve Coxen; Pedro Demo; Jason Dorio; Anantha Duraiappah Mahatma; Liang Du; Gerald Faschingeder; Aslam Fataar; Moacir Gadotti; Chitra Golestani-Maghzi; Sandy Grande; Sondra Hale; Anne Harley; John Holst; Afzal Hossain India; Zhicheng Huang; Liz Jackson; Petar Jandric; Tony Jenkins; Aly Juma; Hyung Ryeol Kim; Sophie Kotanyi; Peter Lownds; Sheila Macrine; Peter Mayo; Lauren Misiaszek; Ernest Morrell; Raymond Morrow; Pedro Noguera; Maria del Pilar O'Cadiz; Irène Pereira; Michael Peters; Adriana Puiggrós; Jevdet Rexhepi; Saajidha Sader; Kabini Sanga; Ilse Schimpf-Herken; Daniel Schugurensky; Lynette Shultz; Graham Smith; Ana Steinbach Torres; Danilo Streck; Rebecca Tarlau; Massimiliano Tarozzi; António Teodoro; Spyros Themelis; Robert Tierney; Richard van Heertum; Yusef Waghid; Sung-Sang Yoo

Freire's Key Terms

EDITED BY
TERESA GARCÍA GÓMEZ

BLOOMSBURY ACADEMIC

LONDON · NEW YORK · OXFORD · NEW DELHI · SYDNEY

BLOOMSBURY ACADEMIC
Bloomsbury Publishing Plc
50 Bedford Square, London, WC1B 3DP, UK
1385 Broadway, New York, NY 10018, USA
29 Earlsfort Terrace, Dublin 2, Ireland

BLOOMSBURY, BLOOMSBURY ACADEMIC and the Diana logo are
trademarks of Bloomsbury Publishing Plc

First published in Great Britain 2024

Series design by Charlotte James
Cover image © Paulo Freire via Torres, Carlos Alberto (2014). First
Freire: Early writings in social justice education. Teachers College Press.
Background image © ilyast / Getty Images

A catalogue record for this book is available from the British Library.

A catalog record for this book is available from the Library of Congress.

ISBN: HB: 978-1-3503-5629-0
       PB: 978-1-3503-5630-6
       ePDF: 978-1-3503-5631-3
       eBook: 978-1-3503-5632-0

Series: Freire in Focus

Typeset by Integra Software Services Pvt. Ltd.
Printed and bound in Great Britain

To find out more about our authors and books visit www.bloomsbury.com
and sign up for our newsletters.

CONTENTS

LIST OF CONTRIBUTORS

Feliciano Castaño Villar. Feliciano is an educator, social anthropologist and Doctor of Education. He currently works as an educator in social services, is a professor at the Open University of Catalonia, a member of the CIMAS Network and the ClaCSO Participatory Processes and Methodologies Working Group and a researcher at the University of Granada. He has published several articles and chapters on anthropological, political and educational topics. He is also a member of the editorial board of the scientific journal *Trabajo Social Global*. fcvillar@ugr.es

César de Vicente Hernando. César was a professor of the Theory of Literature and Comparative Literature at the University of Almería as well as the coordinator of the Centre for Critical Documentation. Previously, he was the coordinator of the Escuela Integral de Arte (1989–2009), of the Sala Youkali (2003–13), and director of the Coordinadora de Asociaciones Culturales de Madrid (2001–15). He was the author of the essays *Gunter Anders, fragmentos de mundo* (2019), *La escena constituyente. Teoría y práctica del teatro político* (2013), *La dramaturgia política. Políticas del teatro político* (2018) and y *La revolución de 1918-1919*.

Enrique Javier Díez-Gutiérrez. Enrique holds a PhD in Education Sciences. He is currently a professor in the Faculty of Education at the University of León, specializing in educational organization. His teaching and research work focuses on the field of intercultural education, gender and educational policy. Among his recent published books are: *Educación* *crítica e inclusiva para una sociedad poscapitalista* (2021) and *La asignatura pendiente* (2020). He is a member of the Seville Forum for Another Educational Policy and the New Educational Policy Networks.

Javier Encina. Javier has been working as a social illusionist since 1995. He initiated and is a member of UNILCO-espacio nómada (The Free University for Collective Construction) and the Collective of Social Illusionists, having coordinated various community participation initiatives, mainly in Andalusia, Mexico, the Basque Country and the Canary Islands. He was a speaker at the World Congress of Participatory Action Research (Cartagena de Indias 1997). Web reference and contact: http://www.ehu.eus/ism and http://ilusionismosocial.org

Carlos Escaño. Carlos is a full professor at the University of Seville (Spain). He holds a PhD in Fine Arts (University of Seville, 1999) and in Education and Communication in Digital Environments (UNED, 2017). His main teaching and research interests focus on art education at the intersection of the arts and audio-visual and digital culture through a critical pedagogical approach and oriented towards social transformation. He has been the coordinator of international cooperation projects conducted in India and Greece and is the editor-in-chief of the journal *Communiars*. He was the director of the documentary *Contramarea* (2016) and the coordinator and author of the books *La otra educación* (2018) and *Lo que no se ve no existe* (2019).

Ainhoa Ezeiza. Ainhoa is a professor-researcher in the Didactics of Language and Literature Department of the Faculty of Education and Sport at Vitoria-Gasteiz (University of the Basque Country). She holds a PhD in Psychodidactics and is currently the principal investigator of the research and training group Seminar of Social Illusionists (ISM), which focuses on participation, education and communication. Web reference and contact: http://www.ehu.eus/ism and http://ilusionismosocial.org

Teresa García Gómez. Teresa is a full professor of Didactics and School Organization at the University of Almería. Her lines of research include co-education; power relations, education and gender; pedagogical alternatives, democratic education and educational innovation; and initial teacher training. Her publications include the editing of *Paulo Freire. Pedagogía liberadora* (2015) and the articles 'Bases del derecho a la educación: La justicia social y la democracia' (2018) and '¿Qué profesional de la educación para qué escuela y para qué sociedad?' (2019).

Ricardo García Pérez. Ricardo holds a Degree in Philosophy. In the 1980s and 1990s he worked in the field of popular education (*Escuela Popular de Oporto*) and adult education (*Consejería de Educación de la Comunidad de Madrid*), in which he has collaborated in various publications and co-authored teaching-learning materials. He has worked as a literary translator for over twenty years.

Alejandro Granero Andújar. Alejandro holds a Doctorate in Education and is a professor in the Department of Education at the University of Almería. He is a member of the HUM-267 Research Group, *Investigación del currículum y formación del profesorado* and the R&D Project *Anatomía del cambio educativo: las escuelas ante el reto de la innovación pedagógica*. He is the author of various works of scientific dissemination on gender equality, the LGTBIQ collective and Service-Learning in the field of education.

Luis Ibáñez Luque. Luis is a secondary school music teacher and deputy director of the IES Carmen de Burgos, Huércal de Almería. He holds a PhD in Education Sciences, his thesis entitled *Democracia, participación y negociación en el aula*

de música: una propuesta de investigación-acción. He is a member of the *Utopía y Educación* network (http://www. utopiayeducacion.com). Luis is a regular speaker at numerous teaching centres on topics such as classroom methodology, inclusion and Learning Communities. He writes the weekly column 'Utopias posibles', in the *Diario de Almería*.

Manuel José López Martínez. Manuel José has been a secondary school teacher since 1991. In 2009, he became a part-time associate professor in the Didactics of the Social Sciences area of the Department of Education at the University of Almería, taking on the role full-time in September 2014. His research lines have focused on the practice of intercultural education, education for citizenship and the Didactics of Social Sciences in initial teacher training.

Saray Martín González. Saray graduated in Primary Education and holds a master's in *Investigación y Evaluación Didáctica en el Aula para el Desarrollo Profesional Docente*. Currently, she is working on her PhD researching Didáctica e Innovación Educativa para una Sociedad Inclusiva at the University of Almería. Her research line lies within the framework of her doctoral thesis on *the advent of happy students*, the first advances of which have been presented at various international congresses.

Jaume Martínez Bonafé. Jaume holds a Doctorate of Philosophy and Education Sciences from the University of Valencia where he was a full professor (now retired). He has been a schoolteacher for ten years and an activist in the Pedagogical Renewal Movements. He has published numerous articles and books on curriculum development, teacher professionalism, educational innovation and policies that control the curriculum. *Another Otra educación con cine, literatura y canciones* is one of his latest publications, of which he is co-author.

Juan Bautista Martínez Rodríguez. Juan is a retired professor from the University of Granada (Didactics and Curriculum). He was the director of the Adult Education Programme of Andalusia, receiving the UNESCO International Prize (Paris, 1987). He was also the coordinator of the *ICUFOP* group of R+D+i projects on the theme of Education for Citizenship, curriculum negotiation, democratic evaluation and ecologies of learning in multiple contexts. In this research line, he has published several books and articles (www.juanbamaro.com) that aim to strengthen the framework of democratic public education.

Domingo Mayor Paredes. Domingo holds a Doctorate in Education and is a professor at the University of Almería, where he is also the president of the Learning-Service Association-UAL. He is a member of the HUM133 Research Group: GAIA (Andalusian Classroom Research Group), and of the R&D project *Anatomía del cambio educativo: las escuelas ante el reto de la innovación pedagógica*. Domingo is the author of various scientific dissemination works on Service-Learning and Community Participation.

Alberto Moreno Doña. Alberto is *jerezano* by birth and Chilean by adoption. He holds a PhD from the University of Granada, Spain. Currently, he is a full professor at the University of Valparaíso, Chile. His areas of interest revolve around the relationship between decoloniality, critical education and school. His latest book is entitled *Jóvenes en los márgenes de las instituciones escolares* (2020). More information at https://albertomorenodona.com/

Jorge Osorio Vargas. Jorge holds a Degree in History and a master's in Education and Pedagogical Mediation. Currently, he is a professor in the School of Psychology at the University of Valparaíso, Chile. He is a member of the CEAAL Advocacy Group on Educational Policies and an advisor to adult-education pedagogical networks. His research topics focus on education and citizenship, new paradigms in education, popular education and social movements. His publications from 1990 to the present can be accessed at https://www.researchgate.net/profile/Jorge-Osorio-3

Felipe Quintão de Almeida. Felipe is an associate professor (II) of the Universidade Federal do Espírito-Santo. He holds a PhD in Education from the Universidade Federal de Santa Catarina, Brazil and a Post-Doctorate in Education from the University of Strathclyde, Scotland. He has experience in the area of education, especially physical education, with an emphasis on school physical education and the epistemology of physical education. More information at http://lattes.cnpq.br/3827408926506567

Daniel Teixeira Maldonado. Daniel obtained his bachelor's, master's and doctorate degrees in Physical Education from the Universidade São Judas. He completed his post-doctorate in the Faculty of Education at USP, Brazil. He is currently a professor at the Federal Institute of Education, Science and Technology of São Paulo. His lines of research focus on school physical education, the curriculum, teacher training and qualitative research.

Rosa Vázquez Recio. Rosa is a full professor in the Department of Didactics at the University of Cádiz. She heads the Research Group 'Política Educativa, Escuela Pública y Justicia Social' (HUM109). Her research lines focus on educational policy, inequalities and innovative practices, rural schools, gender and ethnography/case studies. Her publications include 'El valor de los Nadie' (The courage of the nobodies) (*Revista Márgenes*, 2020) and the book *Reconocimiento y bien común en educación* (Recognition and the common good in education) (2018).

SERIES EDITOR'S FOREWORD:

Reading and Reinventing Freire's Words with Essential Tools

Greg William Misiaszek

This book, edited by Teresa García Gómez, is an essential tool for helping to read and re-read Paulo Freire's pedagogies, theories and philosophies to, in part, unveil the systematically hidden politics of (in/non)formal education that affects our world and the planet overall. Freire had discussed the necessity of literacy tools such as what this short-length book provides here. He was an exacting wordsmith who discussed that education should never be easy but must be rigorous work, be meaningful to students, be utopic rather than fatalistic, and have goals of deepening and widening their reflexivity (i.e. conscientização/conscientization). Only such work in education can lead to students' and teachers' praxis rooted in helping to end oppressions and domination.

Reading is also often difficult, which is frequently positive. Throughout his work, Freire focused on using language and linguistics to be precise rather than simplifying it for easier reading. Freirean literacy calls for reading to unpack the politics of language and linguistics critically. The needed rigorousness of such literacy is discussed in Freire's (1998b) letter below entitled 'Reading the World/Reading the Word'.

> No one who reads has the right to abandon the reading of a text because it is difficult, because he or she does not understand the meaning, for example, of a word such as epistemology. Just as bricklayers require a collection of tools and instruments, without which they cannot build up a wall, student-readers also require fundamental instruments, without which they cannot read or write effectively. They require dictionaries including etymological dictionaries, dictionaries focusing on verbs and those looking at nouns and adjectives, philosophical dictionaries, thesauruses, and encyclopedias. They need comparative readings of texts, readings by different authors who deal with the same topics but with varying degrees of language complexity.
>
> (p. 22)

Several years ago, during conferences in Cancún and San Francisco, Carlos and I initially talked about the Bloomsbury *Freire In Focus* book series – in which this book is housed – we envisioned short-length books that would make Freire's work more accessible to a widened audience. We also saw the series as further reinventing his work through a diverse range of themes (e.g. environmentalism, children's literature, theatre, activism, gender and heteronormativity). However, we did not equate 'accessibility' with being *easier* to read. Instead, the books would provide definitions to the lexicon of the education field and Freire's concepts written by the authors and be saturated with real-world examples. Rigour is still necessary to read the Series' books. This book from García Gómez is a crucial tool for critical reading that Freire discussed in his writings. The book's specific focus on Freire's work helps readers to do vital justice-based work through both his words directly and contextually reinventing his words.

Freire used tools such as this book in various ways. Including his own writing, such as in another letter within his book

Teachers as Cultural Workers: Letters to Those Who Dare Teach (1998b). He utilized a dictionary's definition of 'fear' to initiate his arguments of not allowing fear from difficulties to paralyze students and teachers. He argued that these tools increased the pleasure from reading and the beauty of the written word, as well as both being innately very important. Freire stressed that using literacy tools such as dictionaries and encyclopedias deepens and widens students' 'critical analysis of a topic, [which] is a fundamental component of one's pleasurable task of reading or writing' (p. 22). However, he was dismayed that academia, including the field of education, too often deprioritizes both literacy pleasure and literary beauty. In a conversation with Myles Horton, founder of the Highlander Education and Research Center (Tennessee, USA), Freire expressed his dismay that both aspects are frequently seen as indirectly related to being 'scientific'.

> It has been told [to] us, is it right, that beauty in writing is a question for literature. The scientist is not obliged to grasp the aesthetical moment of language. The more a scientist writes beautifully, the less of a scientist he or she is. For me it is not right. It is a mistake. For me the scientist who is not able to write beautifully minimizes his or her science and falls into an ideological lie, according to which the scientists have to escape from beauty.
>
> (Horton et al., 1990, p. 32)

Although this book in the series could be first interpreted as simply an academic reference volume, it is far from it. It is full of detailed descriptions, examples and stories throughout the chapters, those of Freire's life and how Freire's work is being used and reinvented. In various ways, it encapsulates what Freire was discussing with Horton.

Freire's precision of language and linguistics usage was grounded in contextuality, respecting how words are constructed, deconstructed and reconstructed. Freirean pedagogical practices require respecting students' experiences in how they communicate, the words they use and reinvent, and the linguistic structures they (re-)form (Freire in Horton et al., 1990). Similar to how he stressed that teachers have 'authority' but must not be 'authoritarian' (Freire in Horton et al., 1990, p. 61), delegitimizing students' forms of communication, especially in non-critical ways, is a form of oppression by, in part, being authoritarian.

> [younger students] knew something before coming to the school, and it was important for me in teaching syntax of [the] Portuguese language to know what they knew, because they came to the school with a linguistic competency. We don't teach any language to anyone. Children become competent in a language. After that we can teach the grammar. But language we experience, we create. So I respected the students very much.
>
> (Freire in Horton et al., 1990, p. 61)

He widened this argument well beyond classroom teaching. Friere utilized coloniality theories from scholars such as Albert Memmi, to express how colonial languages sustain and intensify 'linguistic "ex-expressions" consisting of the old linguistic bonds would now deepen into an incarnation of a new kind of "language" or expression: the neocolonial' which needs to be 'radical[ly] breach[ed]' (Freire, 1992, p. 157). Such critical readings of the politics of language and linguistics are essential to Freirean pedagogies, as well as reinventing their usages to express the needs, possibilities and challenges of bettering the world. I would extend this to all of Earth, by utilizing ecolinguistics to counter all forms of domination and planetary unsustainability holistically (Misiaszek, 2022).[1] The unpacking and reinventing of Freire's words in this edited book by García Gómez help to further critical teaching and reading in numerous ways, including crucial praxis that emerges.

There have been various critiques of Freire's words; some valid, but many more not. There are some well-founded critiques of Freire's use of language and specific wording that can be problematized, including being gendered, anthropocentric and overly focused on class rather than diverse intersectionalities of oppressions and domination (see Au, 2009; Au & Apple, 2007; Misiaszek & Torres, 2019; Torres & Yan, 2023). Critics of his work include Freire himself. A fundamental tenet of his work is the *unfinishedness* of human beings that counters *finishedness* that entrenches fatalism in banking education (Freire, 1970). Ontologically recognizing unfinishedness must be rooted in the pedagogical work we do to counter fatalism that perverts so much of education worldwide. Too many scholars only (superficially) read his early and most famous book, *Pedagogy of the Oppressed*, rather than rigorously critique his whole body of work. Freire gave several self-reflexive critiques of his own earlier work and others' critiques of his work, including the following.

> The problem with some of these individuals is that they have read my work fragmentally. That is, they continually refer to my book, *Pedagogy of the Oppressed*, which I published over twenty years ago, without making any reference to my later work (p. 386). … the issue of gender, race as an ideological category did not feature predominantly … particularly in *Pedagogy of the Oppressed*. However, once again as mentioned earlier. my critics should not use *Pedagogy of the Oppressed* as the only measure to evaluate my solidarity with subordinate racial groups, particularly Africans and African Americans.
>
> (Freire & Macedo, 1995, p. 399)

Critical historical analysis of Freire's words, including his contextual analysis on his own, allows for reinvention to emerge for '[t]he old … [to be] capable of remaining new when it remains faithful through time to the experience of original and founding intuitions and inspirations' (Freire, 1998a, p. 41; see Morrow, 2019). This book in the *Freire In Focus* series is an important tool to help guide such crucial reinventions.

Note

1   'Earth' and 'Nature' will be uppercased not ecolinguistically to objectify both. In addition, the article 'the' will not be written with 'Earth' for the same reason.

References

Au, W. (2009). Fighting with the text: Contextualizing and recontextualizing Freire's critical pedagogy. In M. W. Apple, W. Au & L. s. A. Gandin (Eds.), *The Routledge international handbook of critical education* (pp. 219–31). Routledge. Table of contents only http://www.loc.gov/catdir/toc/ecip0827/2008038172.html.

Au, W. W. & Apple, M. W. (2007). Reviewing policy: Freire, critical education, and the environmental crisis. *Educational Policy*, *21*(3), 457–70.

Freire, P. (1970). *Pedagogy of the oppressed*. Herder and Herder.

Freire, P. (1992). *Pedagogy of hope*. Continuum.

Freire, P. (1998a). *Pedagogy of freedom: Ethics, democracy, and civic courage*. Rowman & Littlefield.

Freire, P. (1998b). *Teachers as cultural workers: Letters to those who dare teach*. Westview Press.

Freire, P. & Macedo, D. (1995). A dialogue: Culture, language, and race. *Harvard Educational Review*, 65(3), 377–403. https://doi.org/10.17763/haer.65.3.12g1923330p1xhj8.

Horton, M., Freire, P., Bell, B., Gaventa, J. & Peters, J. M. (1990). *We make the road by walking: Conversations on education and social change*. Temple University Press.

Misiaszek, G. W. (2022). An ecopedagogical, ecolinguistical reading of the Sustainable Development Goals (SDGs): What we have learned from Paulo Freire. *Educational Philosophy and Theory*, *54*(13), 2297–311. https://doi.org/10.1080/00131857.2021.2011208.

Misiaszek, G. W. & Torres, C. A. (2019). Ecopedagogy: The missing chapter of Pedagogy of the Oppressed. In C. Torres (Ed.), *Wiley handbook of Paulo Freire* (pp. 463–88). Wiley-Blackwell. https://doi.org/10.1002/9781119236788.ch25.

Morrow, R. A. (2019). Paulo Freire and the 'logic of reinvention': Power, the state, and education in the global age. In C. Torres (Ed.), *Wiley handbook of Paulo Freire* (pp. 445–62). Wiley-Blackwell.

Torres, C. A. & Yan, L. (2023). Paulo Freire and the state-of-the-art of the international journal of lifelong education. Invited article in celebration of 40 years of IJLE. *International Journal of Lifelong Education*, 1–15. https://doi.org/10.1080/02601370.20 22.2164435.

ACKNOWLEDGEMENTS

This book has been translated into English mainly thanks to the financial support received from the Vice-rectorate of Communication and Outreach at the University of Almeria (Spain), from the Andalusian Classroom Research Group (GAIA, HUM-133) and from the Intercultural Education Research and Evaluation Group (HUM-665).

PROLOGUE

This year marks the centenary of Paulo Freire's birth yet he is ever more absent from the classroom. His work could potentially become relegated to memory even though he is an obligatory reference in the critical education field. Freire had a great influence on educational practice mainly in the 1970s and 1980s, but what place does he occupy today in the planning of initial teacher training? How is his legacy worked into university lecture halls, into continuing education, into the field of social education? Why, by and large, is it not present in these educational spaces or at the distinct educational stages? Looking for possible reasons for this, we can point to different explanations. One of these relates to various aspects of university teaching generally. First, some years ago, the actual teaching carried out at university became of secondary importance as it did not serve to obtain the coveted six-year research periods (sexennials), nor was it the all-important productivity criterion for being placed in the rankings. If teaching is taken as a criterion of the quality of universities, it is only understood and measured in relation to the success rate, to the number of graduates. The attending criteria were not considered – how education contributes to society, to understanding the great problems of our time and then to act on them; instead, the only consideration was how many students passed. Teaching quality is not related to university outreach; it is not understood in terms of the service it provides to society for its own construction, and to developing democracy and social justice. Furthermore, those who consider teaching to be a fundamental activity and who introduce educational innovations into their teaching practice mainly focus on the more technical aspects. There is no deep pedagogical approach with regard to what and why to innovate.

Another possible explanation for the absence of his work might relate to the way technologies have been incorporated into the field of education generally, with education serving them and not vice versa. Pedagogy is relegated to second place, as if technological tools were aseptic tools, turning teaching into a technical issue. As Freire (2005a) remarked when he was in charge of the Ministry of Education and supporting the endowment of computers as they began to be massively incorporated into all schools in the educational sector:

> I don't think education can be reduced to technique, but nor can it be done without it. [...] I believe that the use of computers in the teaching-learning process, rather than being reductive, can expand the critical and creative capacity of our children. It depends on who uses them, for what, for whom and why.
>
> (p. 114)

We find a third explanation in the category of social class – for some sectors social classes do not exist, they are denied; for others, social classes no longer constitute a unit of analysis, talking about oppressors-oppressed is something that corresponds to the past because of the link to Marxism. This denial leads to Freire's work being considered outdated, belonging to a historical epoch that does not correspond to the present.

A fourth reason is related to time management. Applying Freire's pedagogy requires time to think, act, rethink, contrast, discuss, test, contemplate and learn, in a slow and measured way, which directly clashes with the organization and experience of the present, accelerated time.

Lastly, although education was thought about and experienced in collective terms during the decades of the 1970s and 1980s, individualism was imposed on this culture, something unthinkable in Freire's work and impossible to experience in those terms.

The current educational panorama shows a need for and urgently demands a *pedagogy of the human being* (García Gómez, 2015), which is Freire's legacy, in the face of neoliberal education that, regardless of the educational level, has perfected its mechanisms of student segregation and exclusion. This has developed through different processes of domination, oppression and exploitation that continue to be reproduced – seeking merit, personal opportunity and now happiness versus social contribution; continuing to produce the technical-administrative knowledge (Apple, 1997) necessary to maintain the current economy, politics and culture; favouring social control by the dominant groups over the production of knowledge that addresses and contributes to the great problems of our time; turning the Others into deficient or pathological collectives, criminalizing diversity and psychologizing the social and the political; an education situated in technical rationality and an academic perspective, which separates theoretical knowledge from practical knowledge; planning and carrying out the curriculum using the logic of accumulation and demonstration, not for the *potentializing* of individuals and collectives, training human capital rather than educating a critical and active citizenry who construct their own connected lives; turning innovation into activity for activity's sake, doing without a critical pedagogical basis, focused on something to show and not on transforming the educational reality; and reinforcing those controls that maintain the proletarianization and deprofessionalization of teachers rather than the autonomy of those who control the content and process of their own work and their own professional development as teachers.

Given this panorama, *The Words and Pedagogy of Paulo Freire* is conceived as a chance to confront academic and technical education, including university education (which has not yet been broached), in the face of the problems of our time – it asks what type of education professionals to train, for what type of schools and for what type of society?

This book is a collective endeavour that aims to recover the key concepts of Freire's work, interrelated concepts presenting a proposal for Pedagogy, selecting the concepts that allow us to know and understand it, and comprising a sort of practical dictionary. That is why this work is novel compared to other dictionaries, such as the one by Streck, Redin and Zitkoski (2015), which is more like an encyclopaedia in which many of the terms used by Freire are collected and developed theoretically but with no practical illustrations. Our idea for a practical dictionary arose from our desire to produce an operational text, allowing us to connect it to our own practice in a dynamic way. For this reason each term is explained concisely, according to Freire's own conception, and is accompanied by a practical example that illustrates how it has been applied or how it could be applied today. It is a way of showing how valid his legacy still is and offers the possibility of putting his proposal into action, of rethinking it and reworking it in a changed society – as Freire himself did in the books he wrote based on his own practice. To dive more deeply into the selected terms, we have provided references at the end of each concept to the works in which Paulo Freire addressed them in greater detail.

After all the selected concepts have been defined, there is a bibliographic selection of Paulo Freire's works and those written about him. This is extensive rather than exhaustive given his prodigious production. The first part is a selection of his books presented chronologically in order of publication, intended to situate the writings in time, allowing us to contextualize them for greater knowledge and understanding. The second part includes a selection of books and book chapters written about Paulo Freire, his life and his work.

In the line by Freire – today we are doing, tomorrow is yet to be done, the future is not written, this will be our utopia – and, on this, Eduardo Galeano (2004) wrote:

Utopia is on the horizon – says Fernando Birri – I approach two steps, it moves two steps further away. I walk ten steps and the horizon runs back ten steps. No matter how much I walk, I will never reach her. What is utopia good for? ... That's what it's for ... for walking.

(p. 310)

References

Apple, Michael (1997). *Educación y poder*. Barcelona: Paidós.

Freire, Paulo (2005a). *La educación en la ciudad* (3rd ed.). Mexico: Siglo XXI.

Galeano, Eduardo (2004). *Las palabras andantes*. Madrid: Siglo XXI.

García Gómez, Teresa (2015). Editor of *Paulo Freire. Pedagogía liberadora*. Madrid: Los Libros de la Catarata.

Streck, Danilo R., Redin, Euclides & Zitkoski, Jaime J. (Orgs.) (2015). *Diccionario Paulo Freire*. Lime: CEAAL.

Teresa García Gómez

CHAPTER ONE

Paulo Freire

The man who taught by learning
In 2009, the Brazilian government apologized to Paulo
Freire. He could not appreciate the gesture because
he had been dead for twelve years.
Paulo had been the prophet of supportive education.
In the beginning, he taught under a tree. He had
taught thousands and thousands of sugar workers in
Pernambuco to read and write so that they would be
able to read the world and help change it.
The military dictatorship imprisoned him, expelled him
from the country and forbade his return.
In exile, Paulo walked a lot of the world. The more he
taught, the more he learnt.
Today, three hundred and forty Brazilian schools bear
his name.

—Galeano, 2012, p. 374

'NO ONE IS BORN READY-MADE'

—Freire, 2006, p. 314

Paulo Reglus Neves Freire was born on 19 September 1921 in Recife, the capital of the State of Pernambuco in Brazil, into a middle-class family. He was the youngest of four children and was trained in the Catholic religion, which his mother professed. The religious thought of liberation theology ran through his life and in his pedagogical practice and work,[1] and accordingly, he was critical of the church of the oppressors, criticizing the contradiction between the theory professed by it and its practice, contrasting the traditional church with the prophetic church, the latter committed to the process of liberating the human being (Freire, 1975).

Paulo Freire's family suffered the impact of the global economic crisis that began in 1929. He started to fall behind in school, declaring that 'I wasn't being schooled in school, I was educating myself in the world. [...] but I learnt many things outside of school' (Freire, 2006, p. 285). Freire came to this knowing of how to read and write having been taught by his mother and father. He began learning to read the word under the shadows of the mango trees in the house where he was born, writing with twigs alongside his mother in the garden (Araújo, 2001). The house was owned by his grandmother but the family lost it after experiencing economic difficulties. So, in 1932, they moved to Jaboatão, a small town 18 km from Recife (Freire, 1993). The family's economic troubles worsened following his father's death in 1934, which meant that Paulo Freire's brothers and sister, and he himself, had to contribute to the family finances. He gave private classes, with some of his first students being classmates from school (Freire, 2005a, p. 118). He declared it as being a time during which he experienced hunger and poverty (Freire, 2005b).

Thanks to his mother's tireless searching, she managed to obtain a grant for him. He began his secondary education as a scholarship student in 1937 at the Oswaldo Cruz School in Recife, where he studied until 1942 (Freire, 2006). A year before the end of this educational period, the family left Jaboatão and returned to Recife. Freire began to work at the school, first as a discipline monitor and then, in the same year, teaching Portuguese; this he did until 1947 (Freire, 2006). He enjoyed teaching and studying the Portuguese language,

> I was daydreaming. Although awake, I dreamt of becoming a teacher. [...] I was used to 'playing' as a teacher. The intensity with which I imagined being a teacher made it feel like I was. [...] The more I practiced teaching young people like me, the more I became convinced that I was really becoming a teacher, something I loved to be.
>
> (Freire, 2005a, pp. 118–19)

Despite this, in 1943, at the age of twenty-two, he began his law studies at the Federal University of Pernambuco, again thanks to a scholarship, studies that ended in 1947. In his second year at university, he married Elza Maia Costa de Oliveira, a primary school teacher and a public school director. They had three daughters and two sons. Elza actively participated in Freire's projects and greatly influenced his theoretical-practical activity, as Freire himself acknowledged. Encouraged by her, he devoted himself entirely to education, deciding that he didn't want a career in law. He abandoned the legal profession without taking his first case (Freire, 1993, p. 15).

Although he had no initial training in education, Freire was a militant pedagogue in the field of critical pedagogy and his influence was felt worldwide. He himself declared: 'I was becoming a teacher, a process in which I still find myself now. [...] I was becoming a pedagogue, an individual who thought about educational practice and, for this reason, proposed a certain theory of that practice' (Freire, 2006, pp. 314–16). His pedagogy is a proposal to liberate the human being through his praxis (action-reflection-action ...).

He understood education as a human being reading the word and reading the world, a being located in a space and in a time with other human beings, together transforming this world into one where there is no oppression. And, as a situated man, Freire himself began his educational militancy by attending to specific problems in his country, and in Latin

American society generally, engaging in its fight for self-determination and liberation from colonizers. This problem is addressed by Freire in his first work, *Brazilian Education and Actuality* (1959), which he presents as a doctoral thesis while working as a professor of Education History and Philosophy at the University of Recife, and for which he obtained his doctorate in the Philosophy and History of Education. In it, he presented the situation in which Brazil found itself, a society transitioning from a closed society (alienated, dependent on the outside world and on the elite that ruled it, an object that objectifies the human being) to an open society (decolonized and independent, in which the human being and the people are subjects of their own History). It is in this work that Freire makes his proposal to decolonize education, a field he considered colonized, along with economics, politics, culture and theology, proposing cultural action as a political action to problematize reality and thus achieve a critical understanding of it, leading to its transformation through generative words, contrasting it to those cultural actions that aimed to dominate.

His academic thesis, which he would rework and expand on later in his book *Education, the Practice of Freedom* (1967, written in 1965), reflected on his ten years of experience at SESI (The Social Service of Industry), a private institution created by the National Confederation of Industrialists in Brazil, which aimed to assist workers (medically, legally, educationally and in sports). He first worked there as director of the Education and Culture Division and then became its superintendent. During this time, he had the first experiences that led him to develop what later became known as the *Paulo Freire Method*. This began in 1961 within the Popular Culture Movement of Recife, of which he was one of the founders and its first director. Regarding those years Freire declared: 'In my time at Sesi, I learned how to work with the tense relationship between theory and practice' (Freire, 2005b, p. 125).

In 1963, a literacy campaign was undertaken in Angicos, a municipality in the State of Rio Grande do Norte. The campaign resulted in 300 people – 156 men and 143 women – becoming literate in just forty-five days. They came from various occupations – mostly domestic staff, labourers, farmers, artisans, merchants, masons, laundresses, drivers, carpenters and embroiderers – and had diverse motivations for learning to read and write: to improve their life, be a driver, be a teacher, read the newspaper, be a good seamstress, write letters, help others, vote, read the Bible, etc. (Araújo Freire, 2006, p. 139). Because of campaigns such as this, Freire became well known in his own country and abroad. This work led President João Goulart and the Minister of Education, Paulo de Tarso Santos, to invite Freire to coordinate the National Literacy Programme, the objective of which was to make two million adults literate by creating more than 20,000 cultural circles (Gadotti, 1991). This work began by training coordinators but was abruptly interrupted by the military coup on 31 March 1964. Freire was arrested and charged with being a *subversive*, according to the statement from the Brazilian Intelligence Agency. He went into exile at the Bolivian embassy in October. The Bolivian government then hired him as an education consultant in their Ministry of Education, but instead he decided to go into exile in Chile, entering the country on 20 November. This was because, twenty days after his arrival in La Paz, there was a coup d'état in Bolivia. He lived in Chile until 1969, considering this time as the first stage of his exile. A few days after his arrival in Santiago de Chile, he began working as an advisor at the Institute of Agricultural Development (INDAP) and at the Ministry of Education, in the special government office of Adult Education. He was also a consultant to UNESCO through the Chilean Institute of Training and Research in Agrarian Reform (ICIRA) while working as a professor at the Catholic University of Santiago and with the most populist sectors of the Christian Democratic Party (Freire, 1993). The literacy campaigns in Chile, which adopted Freire's proposal and counted on his collaboration, obtained similar results to those already achieved in Brazil. For this reason, UNESCO awarded Chile a distinction that designated it one of the five nations that had most effectively overcome the illiteracy problem.

Freire restructured his method in another context, evaluating its practice and systematizing its theory (Gadotti, 2001), something he continued in his two later works *Cultural Action for Freedom* (1968) and *Extension or Communication? Conscientization in the Rural World* (1969). Freire (1978, 1993) writes that his time at ICIRA was one of the most productive of his exile and that one of the greatest literacy experiences he participated in was that of Chile.

Freire's literacy method was developed exclusively in the field of adult literacy[2] rather than in child literacy. On the applicability of his method to this group, Freire remarked:

> It is basically a vision of educational practice. In the education of children, the important thing is not to open their heads by giving them names of islands and faces, but to make it possible that children might create knowing and know creating (...), expressing themselves and expressing reality in an increasingly lucid understanding of their reality. This is difficult because parents, ideologized by consumerism, demand that their children consume knowledge in school. Universities later transform them into stores of knowledge. Parents demand that schools be small miscellaneous shops for their children. But today there are also spaces for us to change this practice.
>
> (Freire, 1981, cited in Gadotti, 1991, pp. 45–6)

In April 1969, Freire began what he called his second stage of exile, when he went to live in Cambridge, MA, to teach at Harvard University at the Center for Development Studies and Social Change (Gadotti, 2001). In February 1970, he moved to Geneva (Switzerland) to be a special consultant to the Department of Education of the World Council of Churches. This enabled him to visit various countries in Africa (Angola, Tanzania, Zambia, São Tomé and Príncipe, Mozambique) and Latin America (Nicaragua, Peru), participating in their literacy campaigns, advising governments and teaching at the School of Psychology and Educational Sciences at the University of Geneva when he arrived in Switzerland until mid-June 1980, the date his exile ended (Gadotti, 2001).

In 1970, he published his most important work, *Pedagogy of the Oppressed*, although he began writing it in July 1967, the year he gave his first lecture on the subject in New York. Perhaps that is why he first published the work in English, that and the opposition the book received from the Chilean right (in 1969) – the Christian Democratic Party (PDC) accused him of writing a very violent book against Christian democracy. This was one of the reasons why Freire left Chile (Gadotti, 2001, p. 53).

The book was not finished until the following year (1968). Following a friend's advice, he let the text rest and then, on rereading it, saw that it was not finished, and so wrote the last chapter. He discussed the text with various friends, at conferences and at seminars. According to Freire (1993, p. 51) 'I was learning to write it.'

The years in which he was writing the book coincided with a moment in history when global revolutionary processes were taking place – the new left appeared, there was economic globalization and the energy crisis – years in which the civil and political rights movement acquired great strength in the United States, a time marked by the struggle for freedom, when social, sexual, racial and cultural discrimination was denounced (May 68 in France, the Prague Spring, the student movement in Mexico, the Carnation Revolution, the feminist and postcolonial movements, etc.). Freire situated himself in this context and proposed a revolutionary pedagogy with *Pedagogy of the Oppressed*, a pedagogy of the human being (García Gómez, 2015), a way of accessing the world, of being in it and engaging through cultural action with the oppressed, not for the oppressed. This meant, therefore, radical action to liberate and transform the oppressive reality, proposing a problematizing (liberating) education to confront the prevailing banking education.

Years later, in 1975, he accepted an invitation to coordinate a team of educators in the literacy campaign in Guinea-Bissau, carrying this out alongside his team from the Institute of Cultural Action (IDAC). The institute was founded by him together with a group of Brazilian exiles, the aim being to offer educational services, especially to the so-called Third World countries in their struggle for independence. He gives an account of this advice in his book *Pedagogy in Process: The Letters to Guinea-Bissau (1977)*.

At this stage of his exile, he also published compilations of his lectures, seminars and articles, works of shared authorship and others featuring dialogues and conversations.

On 16 June 1980, Paulo Freire returned to Brazil for good, having visited for a month the previous year following a political amnesty, and thus ended his exile. During the 1980s, he worked in the Faculty of Education at the University of Campinas and later in the Faculty of Education at the Pontifical Catholic University of São Paulo. He did not abandon the field of adult literacy since he also supervised the project carried out by the Wilson Pinheiro Foundation, linked to the Workers' Party (Freire, 2009).

In October 1986, his wife died, a severe blow to Freire, who declared 'Elza, an extraordinary woman and educator, whose absence almost took me out of the world, a world to which I returned by the hand of another no less extraordinary woman' (2005a, p. 70). This other woman was Ana María Araújo Hasche, whom he married in March 1988. She later published his posthumously published books and wrote about his life and work.

Freire's militancy and work published from 1989 onwards show him situated in a new context, not only because he had to relearn his country after returning from exile but also, as he declared, because of the global context in which neoliberal policies and public-sector privatization had triumphed. Nonetheless, there was a response by social movements against this neoliberal offensive and the globalization of the eighties and nineties. Freire, faced with the neoliberal project, counterposed it with his own project for a democratic society and education. Again, this was a theoretical-practical project, which began on 1 January 1989, when he became the Secretary of Education in the city of São Paulo following the Workers' Party victory in the municipal elections of 15 November. He held this post until his resignation in 1991, when he returned to his academic activity at the Pontifical Catholic University of São Paulo.

During his time in the Secretariat, he carried out actions aimed at contributing to the literacy of young people and adults, proposing a project called MOVA-SP (Literacy Movement of the City of São Paulo) in close collaboration with the capital's social and popular movements, a project that began in 1990 (Gadotti, 2001). These actions also aimed to democratize the public education system, both in terms of access to education and the educational processes carried out in schools at different educational stages. He gives an account of the work conducted within this objective framework in his book *Education in the City* (1991). This is a compilation of interventions, interviews and texts, as in the books and other works published later, several of which were autobiographical. Some books were published posthumously in which his texts, interviews and letters were summarized; the first, *Pedagogy of Indignation* (2001), was unfinished at the time of his death in São Paulo on 2 May 1997.

Notes

1   It is not the aim of this introduction to give an exhaustive commentary on the life and work of Paulo Freire. For this, you can consult the works of Gadotti (1991), Gadotti and Torres (2001), Araújo Freire (2006) and García Gómez (2015).

2   According to Gadotti (1991, p. 46), it was developed by his daughter Madalena Freire.

References

Araújo Freire, Ana Mª (2001). La voz de la esposa. La trayectoria de Paulo Freire. En Moacir Gadotti y Carlos Alberto Torres (Comp.). In *Paulo Freire. Una biobibliografía* (pp. 11–49). Mexico: Siglo XXI.

Araújo Freire, Ana Mª (2006). *Paulo Freire. Uma história de vida.* Sao Paulo: Villa das Letras Editora.

Freire, Paulo (1975). *Las iglesias, la educación y el proceso de liberación humana en la historia* (3rd ed.). Buenos Aires: La Aurora.

Freire, Paulo (1978). *Cartas a Guinea-Bissau. Apuntes de una experiencia pedagógica en proceso.* Madrid: Siglo XXI.

Freire, Paulo (1993). *Pedagogía de la esperanza.* Mexico: Siglo XXI.

Freire, Paulo (2005a). *La educación en la ciudad* (3rd ed.). Mexico: Siglo XXI.

Freire, Paulo (2005b). *Cartas a Cristina. Reflexiones sobre mi vida y mi trabajo* (2nd ed.). Mexico: Siglo XXI.

Freire, Paulo (2006). *Pedagogía de la tolerancia.* Argentina: Fondo de Cultura Económica.

Freire, Paulo (2009). *Pedagogía del compromiso.* Barcelona: Hipatia Editorial.

Gadotti, Moacir (1991). *Paulo Freire. Su vida y su obra.* Bogota: CODECAL.

Gadotti, Moacir (2001). La voz del biógrafo brasileño. La práctica a la altura del sueño. En Moacir Gadotti y Carlos Alberto Torres (Comp.). In *Paulo Freire. Una biobibliografía* (pp. 50–96). Mexico: Siglo XXI.

Gadotti, Moacir y & Torres, Carlos Alberto (Comp.) (2001). *Paulo Freire. Una biobibliografía.* México: Siglo XXI.

Galeano, Eduardo (2012). *Los hijos de los días* (10th ed.). Madrid: Siglo XXI.

García Gómez, Teresa (2015). Editor of *Paulo Freire. Liberating pedagogy.* Madrid: Los Libros de la Catarata.

Teresa García Gómez

CHAPTER TWO

Pedagogical Concepts of Paulo Freire

Banking Education

According to Freire, *Banking education* (or domesticating education) is the educational approach whereby the teacher (who is understood as a figure of wisdom and authority) transmits the contents unidirectionally to the students (who are perceived as being ignorant) as absolute truths that they memorize passively and uncritically, expropriating the right to think, understand and act on and in their reality. This is presented as static and invariable, so the only possible path is that of resigned adaptation to it and its inequalities. In this way, under the paradigm of supposed objective scientific neutrality, the banking approach focuses on providing descriptions and definitions of reality as something alien to our daily lives, as if the students did not live it, were not part of it, or that they lacked the necessary capacities to learn through analysing it.

The terms in italics refer to other concepts that are collected and developed in this work.

The teacher is conceived as being an authority, in the sense of being perceived as a quasi-divine figure; that is, they are untouchable and cannot be argued with. Meanwhile, students must adapt to assimilate and memorize knowledge unquestioningly and passively. As for the contents addressed, we find that social structures are not discussed but ignored and, thus, they are hidden to reinforce the *false consciousness* of equality, the result of education controlled by the dominant social classes.

All this generates student domestication through imposed adaptive passivity, the domesticating obedience generated from the act of thought control and the unchallenged assimilation of knowledge. Consequently, the students' capacity to transform reality is quashed and it becomes impossible for them to develop critical consciousness, instead favouring their unquestioned accommodation of the world that oppresses them and, through their acceptance and passivity, contributing to their domination by the oppressive classes.

The concept of *banking education* first appeared in *Pedagogy of the Oppressed* (published in 1970) although it was also addressed in his works *Liberating Education* (published in 1973), *Education and Change* (published in 1976) and *The Politics of Education. Culture, Power and Liberation* (published in 1985). However, prior to these works, the author already briefly addresses the domesticating character of banking education in *Education, the Practice of Freedom*:

> Whenever one's freedom is limited, one becomes merely an adjusted or accommodated being. That is why, minimized and severed, accommodated to what is imposed upon him, without the right to argue, man immediately sacrifices his creative capacity.
>
> (Freire, 2002a, p. 32)

Of the works presented, the most detailed treatment is given in *Pedagogy of the Oppressed* and *The Politics of Education. Culture, Power and Liberation*, forming the two reference works in which he gives a complete account of this concept.

In *Pedagogy of the Oppressed,* some original aspects are provided that are substantive when it comes to understanding this approach, such as the loss of the teacher's autonomy and freedom at the expense of the ruling classes' interests, their ability to see and understand reality also expropriated, limited to abiding by pre-established roles, mechanisms and contents. Similarly, the concepts of *adaptability* and the *necrophilous individual* are addressed in detail, both closely linked to the banking concept. Freire uses the latter, in reference to the teaching staff, to characterize those who reach fullness in their relationships with people and reality through the act of possessing and controlling them, turning all the knowledge about them into something mechanical, to the point of perceiving them as if they were inert objects. Therefore, the author, influenced by Erich Fromm, states that the necrophilous person is the one who kills life.

In *The Political Nature of Education. Culture, Power and Liberation,* emphasis is placed on certain aspects that are novel to this work. For example, as part of the background of banking education, Sartre's concept of *knowledge nutritionism* is brought in. This can be defined as the conception of learning focused on mechanically instructing people so as to turn them into great intellectuals, which allows us to know the underlying character of the banking approach. Accordingly, it conceives students as beings who are *hungry for knowledge* yet, in turn, does not recognize the wealth of learning that they possess or can discover autonomously, reflectively and experientially; this inevitably leads to the conception of banking education as the only route for the educational process.

He also describes what, for the banking approach, would be a good student: one who moves away from critical thinking, conforms to the models and orders of those *above* and assimilates all information without question. Conversely, the conception of a bad student is linked to those who are restless, undisciplined, who want to discover for themselves and have a desire to investigate the reasons that lead to the facts studied, who break with the established models, or who denounce the injustices and nonsense of the educational and social system.

It should be noted that the banking conception of education refers to a pedagogical model, not to the ideals that underlie the educational practice itself. Freire points out that this approach is characterized by the transmission of positions, knowledge and discourses in an unthinking, uncritical, mechanical, authoritarian and static way, so that, regardless of the ideological component, it can be present in practices and educational systems of a traditional or progressive nature. An education that does not problematize reality so that people reflect on it, so that they can achieve their own learning, will continue to correspond to this banking approach. Specifically, in *The Political Nature of Education. Culture, Power and Liberation,* he analyses the reproduction of the banking concept of education in socialist societies, affirming that, except for Cuba and China, a bourgeois educational model, domesticating in character, that generated *political illiteracy,* was still being reproduced at the time of publishing the book. In fact, he adds that to know reality scientifically, we must not *tip the balance* starting from our concepts, falling into their distortion; instead students reach knowledge through research, reflection and the construction of their own truth, although it is necessary to start from a committed and critical attitude so as not to fall into a false neutrality.

The great difficulty encountered when exemplifying this banking concept of education has come, unfortunately, from the many experiences fitting this approach at the different educational stages. Out of all of them, the case of a subject taught within the now defunct Diploma of Teaching degree will be examined, although it is only one of many examples that could have been explored here.

This subject is remarkable for the dissonance between the contents studied (The New School, The Modern School, socialist ideas in education, Freire and Critical Pedagogy, etc.) and the approach proposed in it, because, although the contents were especially suitable for problematizing the educational and social reality, reflecting on educational theorization, problem-solving and the discovery made by students in the act of learning, the teacher opted to transmit the contents in a masterful way, explaining it in class with the support of slides, memorizing topics and summarizing the chapters of the work *Education, the Practice of Freedom* (Freire, 2002a) for its later transmissive exhibition to the other classmates. There were no possibilities for reflection, research, analysis or debate of the current or past reality around these pedagogical movements, prioritizing the result rather than the issues that could emerge in the process. Nor was there problematization of the educational reality or the social structures that, both historically and presently, have controlled and have benefited from education (the ruling classes, large companies, the Catholic Church, political interests, etc.). They did not consider the experiences of the students, which were rich sources for understanding the contents, nor did they analyse the educational reality linked to it given their experiential sense. In this way, the students were seen as *empty containers*, with nothing to contribute and without any valid knowledge, as objects that had to be filled with pre-established knowledge from the syllabus provided by the teacher. Therefore, the role of the students was limited to obediently attending to the teacher's explanations, reading to summarize and expound masterfully, as well as memorizing the contents point by point in order to pass the exam, an exam which consisted of writing in detail about one of the eleven subject topics chosen at random, using this as the main assessment instrument. There was no dialogical process in the act of educating, but instead the teacher imparted a monologue towards the students, acting as the wise figure who, in a hermetic and authoritarian way, did not allow any discussion or criticism.

Thus, one of the subjects with the greatest potential for problematizing reflection simply became a tool for the submission, acriticism and domesticating obedience of future teachers, reproducing the banking model of education that Freire himself criticized, and despite being one of the working authors, this fact generated no conflict in the teacher himself.

References

Freire, Paulo (1990). *La naturaleza política de la educación. Cultura, poder y liberación*. Barcelona: Paidós/MEC.

Freire, Paulo (2002a). *La educación como práctica de la libertad* (11th ed.). Madrid: Siglo XXI.

Freire, Paulo (2002b). *Pedagogía del oprimido* (16th ed.). Madrid: Siglo XXI.

Freire, Paulo (2002c). *Educación y cambio* (5th ed.). Buenos Aires: Ediciones Búsqueda.

Freire, Paulo, Fiori, Hernani & Fiori, José Luis (1979). *Educación liberadora* (5th ed.). Bilbao: ZERO.

Alejandro Granero Andújar

Being More

Being more is one of the cornerstones of Paulo Freire's work. If we apply this category of analysis to the human being, knowing this to be unfinished or unfulfilled, we will find an open window to life, a basic objective in one's search to transform reality. Being more human consists of activating a power that allows us to be fully in the world and to relate to others in order to overcome the antagonistic relationship between the oppressors and oppressed. Within the vocation to be more is the presence of the other, in terms of promoting liberation, autonomy and social transformation in the face of oppression, of dependence and of maintaining the *status quo*. In this scenario, education may choose to keep one anesthetized, to be less, or instead apply its transformative tools to be more. For this reason, education emerges as the way forward to humanize the human being, that is, to provoke in them an emancipatory action, because any oppression dehumanizes them, objectifies them, turns them into a *being for another*, thus undoing the possibilities of being more.

Throughout the history of humanity, there has been a collision between the humanization and dehumanization of subjects located in space-time coordinates. For Freire (2002, p. 38), humanization and dehumanization 'are possibilities of men as unfinished beings, conscious of their inconclusion'. This double possibility, of humanizing or dehumanizing, 'is one of the aspects that explains existence as a permanent risk' (Freire, 1973, p. 55). From there, we ask ourselves, why does dehumanization occur at work, in everyday life, in social relations? What force acts to diminish the action of humanizing subjective and intersubjective life and, therefore, educational life?

The answer is that this dehumanization is the 'result of an unjust order that generates the violence of the oppressors and consequently that of being less' (Freire, 2002, p. 39). It is in this contradiction between oppressors and oppressed where the oppressed person can develop praxis, the conjunction of reflection and action, to emancipate themselves and to free the oppressor, since oppressors make it impossible for others to be and cannot themselves be more when they make others less. In this process, and in an education that provides the possibility for the human being to be more, the teachers who accompany the students on this journey of exploration play a prominent role by unveiling the consequences of an oppressive and unjust reality. It is a path along which opportunities arise to forge links between the human being and the community, in this case, between the learner and the educator. This is because a human being is not made alone and cannot be alone; the process has to be undertaken with others, with the community. Freire looks for the nature of the human being – what is their intrinsic nature? In this regard, the historical vocation of the human being is to become conscious of the regime of oppression in which they find themselves in order to act on it, to distance themselves from it and overcome the oppressor-oppressed order that leads them towards being an automaton, that is, 'the denial of their ontological vocation to be more' (Freire, 2002, p. 80).

If we apply the concept of being more to the context of the initial training given as part of the Early Childhood Education

Degree, specifically in the didactics of the Social Sciences (the Spanish abbreviation being CC.SS.), we can transition towards a new outlook, one which is more emancipatory and less domesticated. We can underpin a more critical use of social knowledge in early-childhood classrooms. To do this, we must start from the situation of teachers at this educational stage, their situation of being less. Most of these trainee teachers are female. They find themselves in this context due to a series of limitations that are listed below.

1   Within the educational system of our country, the Early Childhood Education teaching profession is relegated to the lower, non-compulsory levels. There is still no social recognition of the complicated teaching work that takes place at the 0–6 years educational stage even though it is essential for the personal and social development of democratic citizenry, both now and in the future.

2   Most of the university students who approach this specific didactic field come with a preconception of CC.SS., crystallized from previous experiences that were rarely stimulating, experiences we could classify as oppressive because the social knowledge acquired was taught and learnt mostly through a banking conception of education.

3   Another limitation is the difficulty in conceiving that, beyond History and Geography, other social knowledge coexists (which also belongs to the so-called social sciences), knowledge that helps us to understand and transform reality.

4   The trainee teachers lack the necessary competencies for teaching social contents because they do not have a structure and a conceptual framework that suits an alternate teaching of CC.SS., one that surpasses the traditional hegemonic model.

5   Likewise, there is a lack of confidence that is manifested repeatedly by these degree students.

Having started with only a meagre relationship to social knowledge in the pre-university stage, these students are filled with doubts and do not know how to develop stimulating teaching and learning processes from the CC.SS. contents. This anguish arises from not understanding how historical time and geographical space can be covered with children from zero to six years old, and not having had the opportunity to carry out an epistemological reflection on the scientific and school knowledge relating to CC.SS. This is especially the case in History and Geography.

6   In initial teacher training, an adult-centric social representation persists in which children are seen as passive beings into whom knowledge is deposited by the educator. Difficulties appear in recognizing children as members of an active citizenry who must participate in collective decision-making.

Below, we discuss the actions that could be carried out to transition towards a new outlook that is more emancipatory and less domesticated, and suggest how future teachers can use social knowledge. Through their transformative action, future early-childhood education teachers will be able to help their students from 0 to 6 years old to *be more*.

First, reflection and action need to be combined to detect the limitations that make the teachers less and prevent them from being more in a world as complicated as ours. Second, a dilemma will arise – whether to be mere transmitters in the banking education framework or to be agents of social transformation, problematizing and liberating an education that promotes a critical reading of the world. Third, the future teacher will be invited to be more. They will be able to decide, to change their self-concept to one of being an autonomous teacher, to see themselves and strengthen themselves as agents of cultural and social transformation. They will become conscious of the alienation of *being less* in the formal school structure. Fourth, we will work inside and outside the classroom on the possibilities of reflection and action offered by school praxis, as a specific task of teaching identity. With these actions, we aim to strengthen the teaching staff to overcome the pejorative and distorted image that society has created with regard to teachers of early-childhood education. One of the exercises to help overcome this belief will be to recover the dignity lost by early-childhood education teachers in placing them in an imaginary collective conditioned by an outlook that is broadly welfare-based and non-educational. The novice teacher will be offered an exercise in which they have to think about how a tree resembles the teaching profession and, from there, will be invited to paint the tree they identify with, sharing with the class group the reasons for that identification, a representation that will be referred to and considered throughout the course.

Another liberating practice will be to analyse and reconstruct a corseted conception of CC.SS. This provides an opportunity for a minimum level of empathy to emerge that positively predisposes university students to epistemologically reflect on the function of social knowledge today. The reflection will be achieved by verifying the transformative possibility of using this knowledge educationally in a complex world full of inequalities and social injustices. And since the epistemic capacity possessed by the university student is trusted, it will be suggested that they design their own portfolio as an instrument of metacognition and self-evaluation. This will include reflections on the teaching and learning of historical time and geographical space in early-childhood education for students to verify their ability to create professional knowledge and savvy. Along this training path, joint student-teacher work will be essential in analysing the various strategies and methodologies of CC.SS. teaching and learning, both to configure a conceptual framework adjusted to generalist teaching and for the various CC.SS. teaching aims appropriate for the twenty-first century.

Nevertheless, a considerable number of undergraduate students do not understand how historical time and geographical space can be incorporated when working with children from zero to six years old. To overcome this limitation, one needs to describe and interpret the context in which we find ourselves. One recommended exercise is to appreciate ourselves as situated, historical human and social beings, determined by time and space. In this context analysis, students will be surprised to see in practice that time and space, as essential metaconcepts for subjective and intersubjective life, are social constructions, artifices made by human beings to organize socially. The university students will perceive that the context is not static and neutral when dealing with the diversity of the historical time and geographical space in which we find ourselves, and that the infants they teach are in fact the actors that build today's society. In addition, they will verify that Anthropology, Economics, Sociology, Social Psychology, Political Science, Law and Education Sciences are social sciences. In this unveiling, a further possibility will open up – that of focusing education as a critical and problematizing social science, as shown by Freire in his ability to assemble practice and theory into a dynamic pedagogical creation.

However, one of the keys to the transformative process is detecting adult-centrism. We recommend that the degree students evaluate the negative consequences of maintaining a reduced conception of childhood. To do this, one will have to perform tasks aimed at forging a humanizing teaching identity, constructing healthy subjectivity as an adult, and intersubjectivity in the form of a symmetrical relationship with people from zero to six years old. Accordingly, the contents of the United Nations Convention on the Rights of the Child (1989) will be analysed in depth. If we work to unmask those adults who believe they have the authority and right to decide and act without considering the needs and demands of the child students, we will help train teachers to be agents of transformation and to eliminate the repeated perception of the infant as a passive subject. By strengthening this critical consciousness, we will help to undo those oppressive relationships that have remained between adults and infants. To conclude, we can say that incorporating the

Freirian category of *being more* in the initial training of future educators will mean that they do not provoke their students into *being less*.

References

Freire, Paulo (1973). La concepción bancaria de la educación y la deshumanización. In Paulo Freire, Hernani Fiori & José Luis Fiori (Eds.), *Educacion liberadora* (pp. 49–64). Bilbao: ZERO.
Freire, Paulo (2002). *Pedagogía del oprimido* (16th ed.). Madrid: Siglo XXI.

Manuel José López Martínez

Communication

According to Freire, the human world is a world of communication, since it is through communication that we can enter the world around us, perceiving it in an increasingly complex way. What characterizes communication is that it is dialogue, just as dialogue is communicative.

Communication allows us *to admire* reality, that is, to look at it from a distance, to objectify it, grasp it, enter it, and get to know it more and more lucidly so as to discover how the perceived facts interrelate. It is, at the same time, a field of action and reflection, because, by speaking the world, it is transformed.

From this perspective, it would not be a question of analysing communication via an information processing model (sender-receiver-message-code-channel), but of understanding that, for the communicative act to be efficient, it is essential that the subjects, communicating reciprocally, are perceived within a common framework of meaning that makes mutual understanding and recognition possible. When thinking, speaking and acting on reality, communication mediates between reality and the human beings; hence, thought essentially needs the presence of other thinking beings so that the thought is co-participated. There is no *I think*, but rather a *we think*.

The object one thinks about thus becomes the influencer of communication and not its endpoint. With communication, there can be no passive subjects, being a dialogical-communicative relationship between those who are part of it, which helps one to perceive the world in which one lives, in a natural sense, a world that is also culturally and historically intertwined.

Therefore, with communication, there is a union between action and reflection. According to Freire, if there are no reflection and action, there is no communication. For reflection-action to take place as something inseparable, there must be a loving relationship between the interlocutors; that is, there must be faith that there will be bonds of trust between the interlocutors. This is how hope can be generated in social change and transformation. This process of communicative mediation between historical subjects is inseparable from dialogue and education.

In recognizing subjects, one must take into account that human groups and people who suffer or have suffered various forms of historical-cultural oppression may feel blocked or mute. Do not think that their silence is because they have nothing to say, even if they say *I have nothing to say*. If someone has nothing to say, it may be that they consider themselves ignorant, which is precisely due to the process of lived or perceived colonization, or that they are dealing with issues for which they have no references, not being part of their cultural or community knowledge field, or that they are communicating in a foreign language (academic, technical or with the expressive forms of other social classes). Therefore, it is essential to differentiate between silence and mutism, between silent and silenced.

Silence is part of the construction of communication because communication does not consist of continuously filling silence with words to simulate, in an illusory way, a participatory construction. Whoever has something to say must assume the duty of *motivating, of challenging the listener*, so that the listener says, speaks and responds in a way that dilutes the different communication roles down to horizontal and dialogical forms.

Mutism and the culture of silence, on the other hand, come from the fact that the ruling classes have imposed silence on the dominated classes and, once imposed in a historical-cultural way, use it to demonstrate the incapacity or ignorance of the oppressed classes. It is through the gentle handling of language, conscientization and a pedagogy of freedom that effective and thus transformative communication can flourish.

For all these reasons, Freire argues that it is essential not to confuse effective communication with *making communications*, which would be banking education – to think that the people about whom these communications are issued are empty beings that must be filled with information. As long as the educator-learner relationship is not horizontal, i.e. not all the people involved in the educational act are considered as subjects, we would not be talking about communication, but about training or domination, and in many cases about verbosity or verbiage, where whoever makes the communications does so within the time of the vertical relationship, considering the time of their communications more important than the time of the people from whom docility is expected. This would be an anti-dialogical position.

Although Paulo Freire does not substantially modify the concept of communication throughout history, he deepens and interrelates it with other key concepts. He posed the core of this concept during his time in Chile (1964–9) as an exile from the Brazilian dictatorship (Cabaluz & Areyuna-Ibarra, 2020). Starting from concepts such as object-subject or dialogicity, which are present in his work *Education, the Practice of Freedom*, coming from his collaboration with the Chilean government in the agrarian reform process in conjunction with adult literacy and the reform of formal education, all helped him to understand that it was necessary to move radically from the transmission of knowledge to collective construction. The results of this process are contained in his main work on this concept: *¿Extensión o comunicación? La concientización en el medio rural.* From this work onwards, communication, dialogicity and education become inseparable.

Freire's concept of communication influences a number of derivatives and developments, such as the concept of popular communication, of social mediation or the participatory paradigm of communication for social change. It is a key concept in the ways popular educators work, those who want to meet the people of the communities they go to, overcoming communication barriers with the help of a *simplified* language, that is, a language that maintains complexity (not a didactic simplification) thanks to handling the academic language smoothly, woven into concrete aspects of the community. These ways of working began in the mid-1960s in the Brazilian favelas, and became widespread in the 1970s in other places, together with liberation theology and participatory action research, such as in women's collectives for struggle, with workers in industrial factories and in community health working groups.

This way of working is also transferable to formal educational environments, such as the work carried out since 2014 at the University of the Basque Country with groups from the Degree in Primary Education (Encina & Ezeiza, 2018). It begins with a simple question: *What are we going to do during the time we share this subject?* This cannot be a simulated question, but rather a statement of intent to recognize the students as subjects in the process. When that question is posed and the students (or a good proportion of them) *do not think of anything*, something which is usual, we must avoid expressions of guilt such as *the students do not want to participate, they are not involved,* or *young people today are very passive.* All these ideas only accentuate the mutism and distrust of the students who, accustomed to receiving communications and orders, may be suspicious, not believing that they can really decide for themselves, or may feel blocked due to their lack of self-esteem. That is why the educator must provoke various reactions, either using eliciting resources (videos, images, short texts, etc.) or with some dynamic that breaks the verticality and relaxes the environment (e.g. a simple game that provokes a moment of joy or using music). To begin with, it is enough for just a few people to give ideas about what they want to do, thus starting in the simplest of ways.

At the beginning of each session or each week (depending on the frequency of the sessions), what has been done up to that point is shared, the idea being to make the proposals that arise more complex and to interweave the projects. To avoid falling into mass culture or superficial projects that would only extend the lack of knowledge, the following conditions are defined: that each person works on the project he/she prefers, individually or in groups, without predetermining the size of the group; that the individuals or groups who are carrying out a given project help one another and allow themselves to be helped, so that all the projects advance and are intertwined, whenever possible; and that the projects treat all the people involved as subjects (e.g. if a project requires the use of the faculty corridors, there must be intercommunication with the people who use them at that time, such as other students, administrative and service staff, and the cleaners). These conditions are summarized in an idea that is quickly understood: *not to be selfish*, that is, as Freire proposes, passing from the *me* to the *we*. The shared moment at the beginning of the sessions is also used to interrelate the various projects, give them greater complexity and share them, so that anyone can contribute or be part of a project at any time; it also serves as a form of process evaluation.

This way of working differs from project learning in that the projects are influencers of intercommunication, placing the forms of relationship in the foreground and the contents in the background (not that the contents do not matter, but it is more important to help each other and share knowledge). Groups are not closed, group cohesion is not promoted, so intergroup competitiveness, intragroup pressure and endogamy are avoided. Likewise, though the projects are realized, they are modified throughout the process so as to respond to new creativity, since the initial projects are only the first ideas to emerge, and those ideas should not be an anchor or a mandatory task, but merely a starting point (rather a way of releasing the moorings to start sailing). Some people are slow to overcome mutism and communicate only when they feel that the climate is trustworthy, so projects should not be closed in a way that prevents some people from participating as subjects (giving us a false image of participation) while other people continue to be objects, in this case of their own colleagues. Giving time for this is fundamental because, although it may sometimes seem that they are *doing stupid things* (a label that is used to continue stealing the students' self-esteem), when communication is established as Freire conceives it – honest and authentic communication rather than simulated (i.e. saying what the teacher wants to hear) – it is then that collective knowledge construction occurs, a construction dialogued through reflection-action, in which the perception of reality is deepened.

The educator's role in this process is to interrelate the various proposals, value the conversations that arise during the process, help build complex knowledge, critically interconnect the knowledge that is shared with other more academic knowledge, and nurture a climate of trust and mutual care.

References

Cabaluz, Fabián & Areyuna-Ibarra, Beatriz (2020). La ruta de Paulo Freire en Chile (1964–1969): alfabetización popular e influencias del marxismo heterodoxo. *Revista Colombiana de Educación*, 1(80), 291–312. Retrieved from https://doi.org/10.17227/rce.num80-11066.

Encina, Javier & Ezeiza, Ainhoa (2018). Simulacros: trabajando la esperanza de lo imposible en la Universidad del País Vasco. In

Javier Encina, Ainhoa Ezeiza & Emiliano Urteaga's (Coords.), *Educación sin propiedad* (pp. 335–58). Guadalajara: Volapük.

Freire, Paulo (1983). *La educación como práctica de la libertad.* Madrid: Siglo XXI.

Freire, Paulo (1984). *¿Extensión o comunicación? La concientización en el medio rural* (13th Ed.). Mexico DF: Siglo XXI.

Ainhoa Ezeiza and Javier Encina

Conscientization

Paulo Freire explains conscientization as a liberating education process through which people, from their shared daily experience, awaken to the reality of their social situation, advance beyond the limitations and alienation to which they are subjected, and acquire a critical consciousness about themselves and reality. This they can then transform into action, affirming themselves as conscious subjects and co-creators of their historical future (Freire, 1974). Such a transformation requires a process of *decolonization* and overcoming the various forms of *magical* and *naïve consciousness* in order to access a critical consciousness of reality 'so as to better understand, explain and transform it' (Freire, 1971, p. 57). At the same time, it requires one to be involved in 'a practical experience of collective transformation of the world' (Freire, 1975, p. 9), inserting oneself 'in history, no longer as a spectator, but as an actor and author' (Freire, 1969, p. 26), as someone who re-writes the history and destiny of the world (Freire, 1971).

Conscientization is made possible through an organized and intentional process of action and education – what Freire referred to as *cultural action* (Freire, 1975, p. 29) – dialogical-political cultural action through dialogic debate and the problematization of reality that enables one to confront the reference points with which reality is perceived from different perspectives (Freire, 1971). 'Dialogue constitutes the "essence" of revolutionary action'[1] (Freire, 1970, p. 209), which promotes critical participation in the reconstruction of society through the process of conscientization.

Although starting from the political nature of all education, and seeing education as a form of revolutionary praxis, he understands that problematizing educational practice is not enough to liberate the oppressed classes (Freire, 2011) – radical transformation of society is also needed; the educational process alone cannot change society even though it might contribute to doing so. That is why he assumes education to be 'political praxis at the service of the permanent liberation of human beings, which not only happens in their consciousness, but also in the radical transformation of structures, the process within which consciousness is transformed' (Freire, 1974, p. 47).

Conscientization occurs at the level of praxis, as a dialectical relationship between action and reflection, since it involves an awareness of, and at the same time, a critical insertion into a given historical process, which leads to a commitment to transform reality. 'I conscientize myself to fight. Fighting conscientizes me' (Freire, 1987, p. 175), that is to say, an action that critically reflects, and a critical reflection shaped by practice and validated through it.

This approach involves assuming a utopian posture, of progress and continuous improvement towards the *viable unknown* (the future dream that is, at the same time, possible). It therefore requires a permanent dialectical task that reveals the particular oppressive reality in a critical way, along with a historical commitment to a radical liberating transformation of that reality (García Gómez, 2015).

In most parts of the world, neoliberal ideology is defining the focus of current education system reforms: curricula based on competencies, entrepreneurship, standardized assessments, rankings, excellence, competitiveness, etc.; in such a way that discussion in the educational field no longer focuses on how to develop emancipatory knowledge with a critical sense, or how to help the vital development of students by guaranteeing them full citizenship and real participation in the construction of a more just society. Currently, it seems that the dispute focuses on how to orient the curriculum (and the future of education) according to the labour market, the aim being to increase international competitiveness and profit.

The issue of labour insertion takes precedent over aspiring to integrate future citizens socially, vitally and politically. In the school, professionalization is no longer one aim among others but has become the main guideline of all reforms. With the spread of this dangerous neoliberal ideology, there is a real risk of reducing education to those skills that are useful for business, and of obeying a utilitarianism that prevents interest in any education that seems to be unsellable in the labour market. That is why, today, it is more necessary than ever to reorient education by focusing on a conscientizing approach, which means repoliticizing education[2] in the Freirean sense. As Nichols and Berliner proposed (2007, p. 36):

> [W]e should be number one in the world in the percentage of 18-year-olds who are politically and socially involved. Far more important than our math scores and our science scores is the involvement of the next generation in maintaining a real democracy and building a fairer society for those who need it most: the young, the sick, the elderly, the unemployed, the dispossessed, the illiterate, the hungry and the homeless. Schools that cannot produce a politically active and socially useful citizenry should be identified and their failure rates reported in newspapers.

To this end, we must stop conceiving education as being solely at the service of the market and future labour. We should question the banking model with its encyclopaedic curricula, oversaturated with lists of concepts and learning, often disconnected from the social and vital reality lived by the students and their social community – as if school and life were two alien worlds, where you are not educated for life but simply to pass the next exam. One of the possible steps is to rethink the curriculum, and the teaching and learning process, from a conscientizing perspective, starting from the relevant, urgent and vital issues that students are experiencing, their social environment and humanity today, thus allowing them to acquire a critical understanding of the world and help them transform and improve society and the planet on which they live in the service of the common good.

For example, what if we reconvert and reorganize the subjects, looking at the material from another perspective? If instead of organizing the contents into subjects such as Language, Mathematics, Knowledge of the Environment, Music, Physical Education, etc., we convert ecology, coexistence, equality, justice, interculturality, health and quality of life, affections and integral sexuality, caring for other, citizenship, cooperation, solidarity, responsible consumption, etc., into subjects. And, around these *subjects* or materials, we develop all the other instrumental learning of language, mathematics, music, etc. Wouldn't it make more sense to have learning for life, for critically understanding the world and for transforming and improving reality?

Conversely, what if we start by analysing the present to understand the past and how it affects us? What if we begin the History of Spain with recent history, and the proximate dictatorship – Franco's repression and the anti-Franco struggle – which is not usually broached or is passed over *almost on tiptoes*, as research shows (Díez-Gutiérrez, 2020); instead, we start with prehistory over and over again? Wouldn't it be easier to understand the past and how it has shaped the present by starting from the closest reality that students are experiencing?

A third example – proposing an interdisciplinary and globalized curriculum that questions the traditional logic of curricular fragmentation and opts for dialogue and the integration of knowledge and subjects around research topics, or *subjects* of essential analysis, making them more situated, relevant and profound. Instrumental learning would then make sense; it would be functional, serving not so much to pass an exam only to be forgotten later, but to know how to face the world, understand it and act on it by building critical citizenship.

To develop a conscientizing education we need: to introduce a curriculum that is sensitive to social conflicts, inequalities, injustices, climate emergencies and, in general, to the challenges facing humanity; a curriculum that contributes to the formation of autonomous and critical people for global human and ecological development, people who are just and balanced; to emphasize values such as solidarity, degrowth, mutual support and cooperation; to develop awareness, empathy and compassion in the face of human suffering. All of this without losing sight of the horizon – transformation, emancipation, social justice and the fulfilment of human and social rights.

A curriculum that also addresses social, cultural, economic and ecological-environmental emergencies, providing comprehensive schemes and critical analysis that allow one to interpret and act on reality, from a concrete and transformative praxis marked by the common good. Hence, the need to plan an ecosocial, feminist, anti-racist, decolonial, democratic and anti-fascist curriculum in faculties and in educational communities, attentive to denouncing all situations of precariousness that threaten the respect and dignity of life and human rights, in terms of both the proximal experiences of the students and the demands of the collectives and social movements that surround them.

In short, a curriculum that educates about and for life – through critical thinking that interrogates, rethinks and questions the established order, through dialogue and dialogical confrontation of perspectives, to understand a complex and changing world. A curriculum that even calls for disobedience as a legitimate right, which may involve resistance and struggle against laws and norms that are considered unjust, abusive or contrary to the common good (Rogero & Díez-Gutiérrez, 2021).

All this without forgetting, as Freire argues, that necessary educational transformation must be accompanied by changes in the social and political structure, just as this transformation of structures is only possible and lasting when accompanied by the authentic liberation of consciousness. Any truly liberating education must teach the human being to *conscientize themselves*: critically rethinking the world around them and transforming it, bringing together the teaching and learning process with social change for the better, and for the common good. We have to dare to dream and move towards this *viable unknown*.

Notes

1   Although Freire was progressively replacing the discourse of revolution with that of democracy as a way of radical transformation.
2   'Conscientization is never neutral. As education can never be neutral. Those who speak of neutrality are precisely those who fear, in the same way, losing the right to use their non-neutrality in their favour' (Freire, 1971, p. 89).

References

Díez-Gutiérrez, Enrique J. (2020). *La asignatura pendiente*. Madrid: Plaza y Valdés.
Freire, Paulo (1969). *La educación como práctica de la libertad*. Mexico City: Siglo XXI.
Freire, Paulo (1970). *Pedagogía del oprimido*. Buenos Aires: Siglo XXI.
Freire, Paulo (1971). *¿Extensión o comunicación? La concientización en el medio rural*. Montevideo: Siglo XXI.
Freire, Paulo (1974). *Concientización. Teoría y Práctica de la liberación*. Buenos Aires: Búsqueda.
Freire, Paulo (1975). *Acción cultural para la libertad*. Buenos Aires: Tierra Nueva.
Freire, Paulo (1987). *La educación como práctica de la libertad*. Sao Paulo: Paz e Terra.

Freire, Paulo (2011). *La importancia de leer y el proceso de liberación*. Mexico City: Siglo XXI.

García Gómez, Teresa (2015). *Antología Paulo Freire. Pedagogía liberadora*. Madrid: Los Libros de la Catarata.

Nichols, Sharon N. & Berliner, David C. (2007). *Collateral Damage: The effects of high-stakes testing on America's schools*. Massachusetts: Harvard Education Press.

Rogero, Julio & Díez-Gutiérrez, Enrique J. (2021). Currículo humanizador e integral frente al currículo competencial. *El Diario de la Educación*. Retrieved from https://cutt.ly/5n7oJYR.

Enrique Javier Díez-Gutiérrez

Critical Consciousness

The purpose of education, which for Freire can only be a liberating education, is emancipation from oppression through the awakening of critical consciousness, through conscientization. When achieved, critical consciousness encourages people to change and improve their world through social criticism and political action (Freire, 1969).

Moving from a magical or intransitive consciousness, advancing towards a naïve or transitive consciousness and reaching a critical consciousness, the goal of the liberating educational process. This entails not only freeing oneself from oppressive structures and from identifying with the ideology of the oppressor (Freire, 1987), but also seeing the problems from a community and structural perspective, to initiate a process of action and transformation of one's own reality (Freire, 1971, pp. 43–4), based on collaboration and collective engagement, becoming an active subject that makes history.

It is characterized by deeply interpreting problems, by substituting magical explanations for causal principles, by checking the findings and always being willing to revise, by stripping away as many preconceptions as possible in analysing problems and in understanding them, by denying quietist positions, by the security of argumentation; by the practice of dialogue and not of polemics ... ; [it is] characteristic of authentic democratic regimes and corresponds to highly permeable, interrogative, restless and dialoguing ways of living, as opposed to silent, still and discursive ways of living.

(Freire, 1969, p. 55)

Freire points out that the development of this type of critical consciousness has an essential relationship with the educational process as a dialogical and problematizing activity, of critical action-research, which aims to reveal reality in order to place us all (not only the learners, but also the educators) more lucidly and critically in the world: 'critical transitivity, which we reach through a dialogical and active education, oriented towards social and political responsibility' (Freire, 1969, p. 55). An educational process that aims to make the student an active agent of their own learning process and, at the same time, turn the educational method itself into an instrument of conscientization.

It thereby breaks the banking and reproductive schooling logic, while proposing education as a way of becoming aware and transforming reality. Hence, critical education cannot be disconnected from praxis. For Freire, education must place the learner in the world, enabling them to analyse and confront the concrete challenges they live in their context and providing them with tools to transform the socio-economic, political, community, family, group and personal system towards democratization and social justice, openly raising the inevitably political character of education. Education for Freire is an instrument of conscientization, of forming the critical consciousness that is political consciousness. Critical consciousness advances towards political consciousness, for only the latter can make the *untested viable*.[3]

At the University of León we have repeatedly asked ourselves how to help our students develop a critical consciousness in the face of a capitalist system that seduces them into being part of the very system that oppresses them – even going as far as assuming the ideology and imitating the life patterns of the oppressor because 'they fail to see the *order* that serves the oppressors who, in a certain way, *live* in them' (Freire, 1970, p. 63).

> The big problem is how the oppressed, who have introjected the oppressor, will be able to participate in elaborating the pedagogy of their liberation as dual, inauthentic beings. Only when they discover that they carry the oppressor within themselves can they contribute to the birth of their liberating pedagogy.
>
> (Freire, 1970, p. 32)

As an example, we were participating in a rally at the University, called by the university student unions. They had mobilized to denounce being forced to perform free work, where training and work experience were disguised as *extracurricular activities*, to make up for the lack of staff in the university veterinary hospital. What surprised us the most was the reaction of some of the students who obtained one of these places. When we approached them to talk (they had stood facing those participating in the rally) arguing that *they defended their 'right' to freely choose to be exploited* and *who were we to violate their rights and decide for them.*

As the Korean philosopher Byung-Chul Han (2014) puts it, the efficiency of this system basically rests on the process of collective internalization, in which its logic is broadly assumed, adhering *freely* to what one is induced to believe. What capitalism realized in the neoliberal era, Han argues, is that it didn't need to be harsh, but instead to be seductive. Exploitation no longer has to be imposed, we impose it on ourselves and defend it.

Positive psychology and emotional coaching manuals help to self-regulate the oppressive awareness of exploitation and precariousness. To succeed, we are told, what is required is to change our attitude, to get out of our *comfort zone*. Crises are opportunities for those who know how to take advantage of them. Inequality, exploitation and class struggle are now regarded as personal psychological problems (Han, 2021). It is about training, which changes our perceptions rather than trying to change the conditions of exploitation; it is about methods that encourage voluntary servitude.

That is why a fundamental task of all liberating education is the mental and social decolonization of this servitude so as to advance towards a critical consciousness.

> Education can either function as an instrument for facilitating the integration and conformity of new generations into the logic of the current system, or become 'an exercise of freedom', the means through which men and women relate critically and creatively to reality and discover how to participate in the transformation of the world.
>
> (Freire, 1970, p. 15)

In this regard, we are developing the following five strategies outlined below.

Developing a pedagogy of the question. The value and meaning of education are appreciated when knowledge emerges as a response to relevant questions that remain provisional, partial and tentative, to problems that have meaning and are connected to our reality. We try to teach how to question, as Freire (2013) proposed, and to question critically. Developing a critical consciousness is not learning to repeat canned *answers* to questions that we have not even asked ourselves, nor know how they arose or what problems they answered at the time. Instead, a process of enquiry is initiated, of joint critical research between educators and learners in response to the fundamental problems that concern us, taking advantage of the knowledge that previous generations have bequeathed to us. That is why the pedagogy of the question helps us to overcome a model of education that serves only to pass the required tests in the educational institution, that only has a value of exchange for grades and academic titles, and that is rarely useful as a tool for understanding and analysing life, and for critically transforming reality.

This pedagogy of the question is accompanied by a slow pedagogy. It chooses a serene learning process, one that has depth and a slow pace that prioritizes critical reflection strategies, cooperative research and dialogic debate, in contrast to the traditional model of evaluation by results and syllabus advancement by accumulating content. A calm, experiential education, participated in by students who question the culture of quantity and accumulation, an education that prevents the desire to learn being transformed into a simple desire to pass exams.

Both strategies simultaneously demand a pedagogy that is democratic and participatory. Democracy that is learnt is the one that is lived. This is achieved through the dynamics of the classroom, through assemblies, or the students' participation in selecting the contents, methodology and evaluation criteria, or on agreeing the rules and operation of the class and the education centre. We try to go beyond the *liberal democracy* model implemented in education systems through representative bodies, instead moving towards a participatory democracy where students participate not only in finding solutions but in debating and deciding what the problems are, intervene in deciding the economic budgets in a participatory way, which involves a process of critical and political literacy.

A fourth strategy we are developing is to reconnect the education centre with the social community, opening it up to community participation and involving local entities and social movements. At the same time, the centre also engages with the social environment and the community in cultural and social activities, with neighbourhood associations, tackling research and studies of common interest for the neighbourhood and for the environment, cooperating in common projects that have a social impact.

The fifth and final strategy is the pedagogy of mutual support and cooperation, which provides the framework for all the above. That is, to educate others and educate ourselves in how to cooperate rather than compete. Faced with the story of the self-made *neoliberal subject,* competitive and individualistic, who owes nobody anything and who seeks *success* for the sake of self-enrichment, spread through the mantra of the entrepreneur, we instead promote a pedagogy of cooperation and solidarity, which makes us aware of the need for mutual help, common care, solidarity and social justice, without which we cannot survive as a species or as a planet. This pedagogy is imparted not only through the praxis of cooperative education in the classroom, but also in the work dynamics of the teaching professionals, in research, and in the relationship between schools, universities and educational administrations. For example, we intend to move from competitive campuses of excellence to cooperative campuses of mutual support, where knowledge is shared freely and where one is trained in cooperation, knowledge-sharing and copyleft instead of patents, copyright and business creation, with discoveries based on the knowledge of the entire scientific community. All of this means radically changing the culture of competition that populates our educational model.

That is why Freire's pedagogy is today a revolutionary pedagogy, more necessary than ever, since its objective is radical and critical: not only revealing the mechanisms of oppression but, simultaneously, committing ourselves, through liberating praxis, to its transformation (Freire, 1970, p. 53). This is the current priority, the urgent and essential task of emancipatory pedagogy that goes beyond the act of teaching-learning, since it supposes a way of accessing the world, of being in it, of relating in a critical and transformative way.

Note

3   The future dream that is possible at the same time.

References

Freire, Paulo (1969). *La educación como práctica de la libertad.* Mexico City: Siglo XXI.

Freire, Paulo (1970). *Pedagogía del oprimido.* Buenos Aires: Siglo XXI.

Freire, Paulo (1971). *¿Extensión o comunicación? La concientización en el medio rural.* Montevideo: Siglo XXI.

Freire, Paulo (1987). *La educación como práctica de la libertad.* Sao Paulo: Paz e Terra.

Freire, Paulo & Faundez, Antonio (2013). *Por una pedagogía de la pregunta.* Buenos Aires: La Aurora.

Han, Byung-Chul (2014). *Psicopolítica.* Barcelona: Herder.

Han, Byung-Chul (2021). *La sociedad paliativa.* Barcelona: Herder.

Enrique Javier Díez-Gutiérrez

Cultural Action

Freire conceives culture as being the product of human experience. This culture conditions the knowledge and actions that we live socially. Hence, he proposes analysing culture by posing it as an object of reflection to help us be freer. Accordingly, when he speaks of Cultural Action, he is referring to a deliberate and organized proposal, to a project intended to change the concrete situations and conditions of our lives that prevent us from acquiring autonomy and freedom. *Becoming conscious and acting on practice* are inseparable constituents of the liberating transformative cultural act.

Freire requires different forms of cultural action to clarify those situations and conditions that are related to the activities that concern us: work, leisure, social relationships, use of natural resources and the values that determine them. To do this, he draws on the existence of two antagonistic forms.

The first, *cultural action for freedom,* arises from oppressed groups as their own cultural identity and as political organization. This proposal utilizes the scientific understanding of reality, the knowledge of which allows them to unmask internalized myths and the alienating power of ideologies in order to understand the truth of their own reality. Through his methodological approach, living conditions are problematized and, through dialogue, consciousness arises amongst the people, who live in a conflictive dilemma between feeling subject to their living conditions and taking the opportunity to make decisions and be free. Cultural action becomes a dialectical, controversial and continuous experience in the process of making conscious decisions.

The second, *cultural action for domination,* is typical of the oppressors, who resist dialogue and use it to tame the people. They use watchwords, slogans and deception, which are developed through ideological imposition that sabotages and conditions the subjects' thinking. There is an epistemological condition that differentiates cultural action for freedom from cultural action for domination, precisely concerning the utopian nature of the former (Freire, 1970, p. 70).

At this point in his work, Freire goes a step further and strategically claims the political union of the *oppressed* as being indispensable to all cultural action (Freire, 1970, p. 230). As with education, cultural action is characterized by assuming the political dialectic in which the oppressed jointly experience cultural domination and liberation, simultaneously and antagonistically. Freire is convinced that, in this way, it is possible to change situations of domination and progressively overcome the alienating cultural forms themselves, until cultural revolution is achieved (Freire, 1975, p. 236). Consequently, Freire does not draw a distinction between cultural action and cultural revolution; both are committed to conscientization and both, he explains, need the dialectic of *overdetermination.* He uses this analytical tool to explain how a situation of domination can be the effect of several sufficient conditions.

With the intention of clarifying the most important moments of cultural action, Freire characterizes a first phase in which the practice of freedom is applied as a set of alternatives to the dominating power of the elite, while, in a more advanced phase, cultural action is presented within the framework of, and in syntony with, cultural revolution. It should be noted how Freire evolves and revises the different cultural revolution models throughout his work.

Due to the transcendence and impact it has had, we must consider the methodology proposed for cultural action, which, in his initial works, is that of *political-pedagogical literacy*. To theorize and justify it epistemologically, part of the anthropological distinction between the cultural world and that of nature, is that the latter is composed of the environment in which all of us interact and socialize. To work in an operational way, Freire proposes starting from *existential situations* of practice, presented auditorily, visually or orally, the task consisting of having a dialogue on these provocative vital situations in groups and culture circles, and to make them understood through their cultural decodification (Freire, 2009, p. 76).

In these literacy processes, cultural action opens up the meaning of education to go beyond the mechanical and purely technical training of peasants or urban workers, to increase the people's level of political consciousness. Freire guides the forms of cultural action and justifies them by their usefulness in improving economic productivity, which can be all the greater the clearer the political consciousness of the popular masses (Freire, 1978, pp. 109–21). He charts his cultural theory with very common elements and with intertwined concepts; that is why in his work, he consistently insists on talking indistinctly of education, cultural action and animation, since for him such concepts always imply a certain theory of knowledge put into practice by human beings about the contradictory objective reality that conditions them.

On the other hand, it is necessary to consider the roles of the intervening agents or mediating protagonists in the problematization of significant issues for the community and, although this is dealt with more deeply in other concepts, Freire assigns an important role to social workers, educators and professionals in developing the forms and methodology of cultural action. Among many other practical suggestions, Freire is concerned with orienting practical education within experimentation, connection and dialogue between leaders and people (Freire, 1975, p. 76). Thus, the varied methodological propositions of the Culture Circles are developed starting from the basic assumption that culture is the axis or place where liberating education is hybridized in popular culture; this is then built upon and transformed into *cultural action for freedom*.

Freire's permanent and progressively reflective demand to exercise his educational practice in multiple contexts, experimenting and dialoguing with the agents of other conditions and political frameworks, allowed him to revise his initial ideas through the rereading of his theses in terms of the nature of culture and the definition of cultural action. In this line of reflection, influenced by the emerging debates around the existence of different cultural identities, he tries to respond to this complex issue by proposing a political-educational praxis of dialogue between the cultures and identities of differentiated minorities, fighting for unity in diversity.

In his later publications, cultural action under these conditions acquires a new meaning in the modernity-postmodernity discussion; this is because he is convinced that multiculturalism involves the coexistence of different cultures in the same space. In this new context of debates on the ontological dimension of cultural practices, Freire takes up his initial idea of culture as a historical creation that requires decision, political will, mobilization, organizing each cultural group around a common purpose, and a new ethic of respect for diversity. Therefore, the need for cultural action groups persists, although a new ethic based on respecting differences is required, having *unity in diversity* as its central idea, and oriented towards the struggle against liberal democracy and how to overcome it (Freire, 1993, p. 150).

The basic principles and methodological criteria that Freire promoted in his proposal for cultural action, which were applied in cultural circles (among other experiences), have subsequently been shared in a very significant variety of educational and cultural projects.

This is the case with the Medialab-Prado experience,[4] which has emerged from the current context whereby ubiquitous technological tools contribute to the free-access-to-knowledge philosophy and to collaborative work made possible in the network society, a theory that favours connecting other European and Latin American collaborative networks.

This citizen laboratory is dedicated to gathering together and promoting open cultural projects in a space where critical and creative dialogue is encouraged and where any citizen, who always knows and ignores things, can organize themselves into groups to elaborate cultural products, knowledge or resources related to their practice. The shared realization of the projects covers various dimensions, on topics such as citizen participation, resolving environmental issues and finding solutions to common problems. All of these projects are carried out within the framework of ethical-political reflection and in a mutual teaching-learning relationship.

Any citizen can make proposals or join with others to carry them out collaboratively, alongside the *animators* or mediators who bring together, help, guide and take care of the working groups. The richness generated from the participants belonging to different groups, professions, contexts and conditions allows knowledge to flourish within a theoretical framework based on the ecology of learning.

The laboratory's experimental dimension allows communities of learning and practice to be constructed, which favours relationships fostered in a climate of respect and care, thus enabling the sum of multiple contributions to a collective intelligence. The *domestication* and *invisibilization* of technologies are opening up new possibilities for turning other contexts and scenarios into learning laboratories.

Freire's liberating social transformation has been seen as key in contexts emerging from other cultural concepts and practices, such as in social innovation, in which creative solutions to various social problems are developed. This laboratory really has an experiential sense (a living lab) that uses ICT within the network-society-for-sustainability framework, capable of self-training in the design of sustainable communities based on recognizing our common existence and the need to manage our common good dialogically.

Note

4   For more information, see: https://www.medialab-prado.es.

References

Freire, Paulo (1972). *Sobre la Acción Cultural*. Santiago de Chile: ICIRA.

Freire, Paulo (1974). *Pedagogía del oprimido* (12th ed.). Buenos Aires: Siglo XXI.

Freire, Paulo (1975). *La acción cultural para la libertad y otros escritos*. Buenos Aires: Tierra Nueva.

Freire, Paulo (1978). *Cartas a Guinea-Bissau. Apuntes de una experiencia pedagógica en proceso* (2nd ed.). Madrid: Siglo.

Freire, Paulo (1984). *La importancia de leer y el proceso de liberación*. Madrid: Siglo XXI.

Freire, Paulo (1990). *La naturaleza política de la educación. Cultura, poder y liberación*. Barcelona: Paidós/MEC.

Freire, Paulo (1993). *Pedagogía de la esperanza: un reencuentro con la Pedagogía del oprimido*. Mexico: Siglo XXI.

Freire, Paulo (2005). *Cartas a Cristina. Reflexiones sobre mi vida y mi trabajo*. Mexico: Siglo XXI.

Freire, Paulo (2008). *El grito manso* (2nd ed.). Argentina: Siglo XXI.

Freire, Paulo (2009). *La educación como práctica de la libertad* (Revised edition). Madrid: Siglo XXI.

Freire, Paulo (2012). *Pedagogía de la indignación. Cartas pedagógicas en un mundo revuelto*. Buenos Aires: Siglo XXI.

Juan Bautista Martínez Rodríguez

Cultural Circle

In Paulo Freire's vast and extensive work there is a transversal basic thesis: for all those oppressed, whether because of their class, cultural or any other status, education must be an instrument of liberation. But this liberating condition depends on equipping ourselves with procedures that help us to learn the political practice of emancipation during the education process. A practice that, whilst political, is also a collective and intersubjective process. Throughout the discourse of popular education movements with Freirian roots, emancipatory education incorporates the willingness to criticize, which ensures advances in knowledge and culture acting as an emancipatory tool, both for the subjects and for the peoples (Freire, 1990, 1991). The discourse's statements and agenda are nourished by issues such as the education of critical subjects, respect for minorities and the recognition of cultural diversity, developing democracy, fostering participation in the design and ways of managing public affairs, promoting relations between the community and the school, and understanding the school as a public community project.

Within this discourse on popular and emancipatory education, the *culture circle* concept emerges: a practical and theoretical process by which we build and re-evaluate knowledge by reflecting on the multiple objective and subjective aspects that make up and regulate our experience; a process of problematization and critical investigation of our own life experience. A process we carry out together, born from a willingness to cooperate and engage in dialogue between equals, from the historical need to *speak the world in our own words* (Freire, 2005, p. 105) Indeed, the central idea is to give the floor to those who were always silenced. The themes/problems are chosen by the participants themselves and discussed from within their culture and their lived experience. The problems of the world, of society and of our realities are opened up for social actors to dialogue with each other. In this way, liberating education is a pedagogy of the oppressed because it is the oppressed themselves, as long as they discover themselves as such, who provide the body and the voice; it is they who critically reconstruct the prevailing social realities, bringing forth critical consciousness.

In his book *Pedagogy of the Oppressed,* which was edited multiple times, Freire (2005) presents an alternative didactic methodology that is concretized in the culture circle: a space and time for social actors to fully express their points of view, concerns, opinions and their lived problems through circular dialogue, allowing them to develop the collaborative experience of reworking the world and constructing new conceptual categories to become aware of their oppressed condition. Paraphrasing a well-known quote from Marx in *The Holy Family*, Freire tells us that oppression becomes even more oppressive by adding to it the consciousness of oppression, and that this infamy becomes even more shameful when it is proclaimed (p. 49). The culture circle is therefore the public place in which we speak to ourselves from ourselves, feeling ourselves to be subjects speaking out while planning transformation, despite our enslaved condition as objects.

> By objectifying their world, the person learning to read and write is reunited in it, reuniting *with* the others and *within* the others, the companions of their small 'culture circle'. They all meet and re-meet in the same common world and, from the coincidental intentions that objectify them, communication arises, a critical dialogue that encourages the circle participants. So together they critically recreate their world: what used to absorb them, they can now see from the other way round. Strictly speaking, nothing is taught in the culture circle but rather learnt with a 'reciprocity of consciences'; there is no teacher, but a coordinator, whose function is to provide the information requested by the respective participants and foster favourable conditions for the dynamics of the group, minimizing their direct intervention in the course of the dialogue.
>
> (Freire, 2005, pp. 12–13)

Dialogue, the communicated word, is the fundamental tool of critical literacy: through the *codification* and *decodification* of the word, we signify our context and do so with the communicative intentionality of knowing ourselves, together with others, in an education process that liberates us and emancipates us from the processes of objectification.

Here, we must ask a double question – who drives the culture circle? – and also – which subject drives the culture circle to do what? – the response to which makes us re-examine the concept of the educator. In the culture circle, no hierarchies are possible, nor any separation or roles that establish hierarchies. We all constitute ourselves as subjects and, thus, the educator is a *dynamizer* in a horizontal relationship between equals, a facilitator of information and documentation, who establishes the conditions for fruitful conversation in which their direct intervention is minimized. The circle coordinator must be an educator with the intellectual humility and wisdom to listen while recognizing the capacity – the power of action – of each social subject to produce, together with others, a process of co-investigation, in which diverse subjects, with diverse knowledge and experiences united by an ethical relationship, govern their own knowledge production. 'Revolutionary leaders, who dialogue with the people and are in communion with them,' Freire tells us (1975, p. 88). The circle ends up producing its own textuality, through different techniques of collective writing. But in Freire's reflection this is not a methodological response, it is the response to a call for ethical responsibility in performing the teaching task. An ethic that is inseparable from what we do, from our practice and from the meaning we want to give to our educational practice (Freire, 1975, p. 2004).

The conversation and dialogue are extended and qualified using thematic analysis, in a continuation towards what Freire calls *thematic research circles*, a more elaborate phase of the circle, a process of decoding, which challenges the participants – problematizing the codified existential situation, on the one hand, and the answers they themselves give throughout the dialogue on the other. This is a level of *theorization* in which we try to identify and understand the historical and structural character of our practice and the ways in which each of us live it.

It should be noted that this proposal links different traditions of teacher training, critical pedagogy and popular education, arriving at common ground even though they originate from different contexts, cultures and policies. I refer to the action research proposals and the so-called teacher-as-researcher movement, as developed in the Anglo-Saxon context in the early 1970s (Elliot, 1994), in the systematization of the experience strategy born in the popular education projects of the late 1960s and early 1970s in various Latin American countries (Fals-Borda, 1991; Miscellaneous Authors, 1998; Núñez, 1989), and in the cooperative work of the Pedagogical Renewal Movements (PRM), also originating in the 1960s and 1970s in countries such as Portugal, France, Spain and Italy (Martínez Bonafé, 2000). It also coincides with a more recent approach that, based on these traditions and other experiences of social research participation, develops the theoretical and practical idea of militant co-research (Malo, 2004).

In the Spanish State, the Summer Schools of the Pedagogical Renewal Movements were promoted in the middle of Franco's dictatorship. In this context of reflection, analysis and criticism, carried out by teachers dissatisfied with their initial training and committed to political change, horizontal spaces were cultivated for meeting and exchanging knowledge and experiences; these empowered the teaching teams to confront the difficulties of their practice and the political conditions regulating the workplace. In this space, there were certain conditions that borrowed from Paulo Freire's postulates and proposals on the culture circle: the condition of plurality and cooperation between those who know themselves to be equal; the condition of dialogue from recovering one's own word, a dialogue in which concrete problems are signified and the knowledge cultivated in one's own practical experience is exchanged and given away; and the condition of word truth, achievable when one is not dependent on substitute discourses but instead committed to problematizing one's practice and advancing its qualitative transformation (Freire, 2005, p. 106).

A fourth condition, coinciding with Freire's proposals, and those of the Pedagogical Renewal Movements, had to do with the knowledge claimed and the beings produced, with the meaning and usefulness of the teacher's practical professional knowledge. On the one hand, knowledge was shared for the optimal didactic outcome within the classroom and the school, knowledge produced by problematizing and investigating classroom and school situations. But this didactic knowledge was inseparable from another complex set of knowledge areas, those, according to Freire, that would be generated from values of solidarity, social justice, denunciation of any form of oppression and a commitment to transformation. The anti-Franco character of many Summer Schools was not accidental, it was a condition *sine qua non* of the meaning that was attributed to teacher training: teachers who committed their time and had the capacity to develop strategies for change and social transformation, both in their militancy on the street and in their pedagogical militancy.

Although the Summer Schools went into decline, there are many education centres and educational levels where the stamp of the teachers' militant work for pedagogical renewal has been planted. There are schools who owe much to the experiences promoted by the teachers of the PRMs, schools with democratic management, family and community participation, curricular research, no textbooks, assessments that do not contribute to selection and social discrimination, and where the students are recognized as subjects. There are *restless* schools that, through this renewing pedagogy, are promoting a way of thinking and saying how a more just and egalitarian society is possible. In another text, I called this alternative to the teacher being professionally alienated from the *militant desire*. I refer to the will to create our own situations, to make our own decisions. In teacher training, this means that the teacher is aware of their insufficient initial training and that the poverty of routine practice must be replaced by a search for other knowledge, that a research situation is created, a situation that problematizes practice and asks questions. For this to happen, a different knowledge process is required to answer them. As one can imagine, this desire is closely linked to a search for identity – a redefinition of the collective identity of the teacher – and so it must be conceived as a political practice, to wanting *to be a teacher* who conquers professional spaces colonized by alienation. Liberating the word – the word of those who speak so much – to put it at the service of subjectivity (Martínez Bonafé, 2010).

Freire said that we are walking, and I wonder now what moves a teacher to go against the wind of neoliberal individualization and conservative passivity, towards the convocation of a culture circle. Again, with Freire's help, I assert that the answer is the desire to exchange views and reflections on the lived experience, the desire to choose and discuss the themes, carrying out one's own research and learning agenda. The willingness to submit one's own experiential interpretations to public dialogue and critical reflection while contributing to a public memory with textual production that revises the meaning of education within the framework of a just society.

References

Elliot, John (1994). *La investigación-acción en educación*. Madrid: Morata.

Fals-Borda, Orlando (1991). *Action and knowledge: Breaking the monopoly*. New York: Apex Press.

Freire, Paulo (1975). *Acción cultural para la Libertad*. Buenos Aires: Tierra Nueva.

Freire, Paulo (1990). *La naturaleza política de la educación*. Barcelona: Paidós/MEC.

Freire, Paulo (1991). *La educación en la ciudad*. Buenos Aires, Argentina: Siglo XXI.

Freire, Paulo (2004). *Pedagogía de la autonomía. Saberes necesarios para la práctica educativa*. Sao Paulo: Paz e Terra.

Freire, Paulo (2005). *Pedagogía del oprimido* (35th ed.). Mexico DF: Siglo XXI.

Malo, Marta (Ed.) (2004). *Nociones comunes. Experiencias y ensayos entre investigación y militancia.* Madrid: Traficantes de Sueños.

Martínez Bonafé, Jaume (2000). *Trabajar en la escuela. Profesorado y reformas en el umbral del siglo XXI.* Madrid: Miño y Dávila.

Martínez Bonafé, Jaume (2010). Aprender el oficio docente sistematizando la práctica. In Ángel Pérez Gómez (Comp.), *Aprender a enseñar en la práctica: Prácticas educativas y procesos de innovación y mejora en la educación secundaria* (pp. 101–20). Barcelona: Graó.

Núñez, Carlos (1989). *Educar para transformar, transformar para educar.* San Jose, Costa Rica: Alforja.

Various Authors (1998). *Investigación Acción Participativa.* Havana: Pedagogues Association of Cuba.

Jaume Martínez Bonafé

Cultural Extension

Freire proposes to begin reflection from the semantic analysis of the term 'extension' and its associative field, which leads us to understand that extension is transmission – that is, extending something to someone. This means that there is an active subject (the one who extends), a content (which is taken up by the one who extends) delivered (taken to the *other side of the wall*) to someone (the indirect object) who is the depositary of what is delivered. This semantic analysis shows that it is a messianic action of the one extending, who, from his position of superiority, imposes his knowledge on those who must passively receive his message.

From his definition, the intentionality of the extending actions and the work of the extending agent are clear, so one cannot expect such actions to be liberating educational tasks. The extending agent does not see the learner as a subject, but as an object. For this reason, Freire relates extension to cultural invasion, a concept that is found in the same associative field, since the extending agent does not spend time understanding what the person who receives his knowledge knows, considering them ignorant. Moreover, he considers it a waste of time to work in a dialogical way and does not expect to learn anything himself in this process, or to modify his knowledge.

Freire problematizes the term 'extension' as opposed to the term 'communication', the latter being truly educational. The extending agent gets to control and order popular cultures, the knowledge of which, according to him, is dark and magical, based on false beliefs. However, according to Freire, whatever the human knowledge may be, it always responds to a theory about the world that comes from real action, whether we know how to verbalize what that theory consists of or not, since theory and practice are something inseparable. Thus, he proposes that the subject can get to know and acquire new theoretical meanings through practice, and practice, in turn, can help to illuminate the theory to appropriate and deepen it. Hence the importance of maintaining a dialogical attitude that facilitates these processes of individual, group and collective construction.

When the extending agent states that he does not have time to build knowledge in this way, but that it is more effective to work in an anti-dialogical manner, this really means that he intends to culturally invade the community into which he goes, through slogans, propaganda and other tools that place the invaded people in a position of docility, which means taking away meaning from the invaded culture, breaking its character, fragmenting it and penetrating it with by-products of the invading culture. Even if it seems that his action is innocuous because he has not managed to adequately transmit the knowledge and techniques he intended, his action has caused a fracture in personal, group and community self-esteem, by making learners feel useless and ignorant.

As soon as the extending agent identifies himself as *an agent of change,* he has already taken an invading position, because his purpose is to deposit his change, so the more active the agent and the more passive and docile those who receive his deposits, the more quickly he will do his job. It is what Freire calls *alienation of ignorance*, which consists of thinking that the ignorant are the others (the peasants, the day laborers), who are considered a problem because they do not want to learn or do not understand the message that the agent wants to transmit.

Freire considers that one of the great dangers of welfare (sometimes expressed as *coming to help*) is part of the violence of anti-dialogue, which imposes mutism and passivity, instead of offering special conditions to develop or *open up* consciousness to becoming increasingly critical. By deciding what content they should know and how they should know it, we are impeding their knowledge practices and robbing them of the autonomy of knowing how to learn. In addition, we prescribe standardized and delocalized content that is imposed on them. When we do this, we are actually reproducing domination, no matter how revolutionary or valuable the content we try to convey.

The concept of extension and cultural invasion was developed by Freire at a time when the Alliance for Progress (1961–70), with J. F. Kennedy at the helm, intended to eliminate the risk of insurgency and revolution in Latin America by promising *to improve the lives of all the inhabitants of the continent* (the *revolution in freedom*), for which it was necessary to reach those places labelled as *underdeveloped* and educate in ways of life that accorded with the capitalist system, breaking the different forms of resistance of rural popular cultures mainly through family planning, mass literacy and the incorporation of technology into rural production. Freire's successful experience in literacy in Brazil was key to the Chilean government welcoming him into exile from the Brazilian dictatorship and appointing him as a collaborator in agrarian reform, adult literacy and formal education, all within this plan.

Although Freire was initially part of this process, he soon questioned it after interconnecting with groups and movements that perceived it as insufficient reformism, something that would not help the emancipation of the oppressed. Thus, in the main work in which he develops these concepts: *¿Extensión o comunicación? La concientización en el medio rural*, written in Chile in 1968, he denounces the extension agronomists, who are granted the role of subject, extending knowledge and techniques to the peasants, whom they treat as objects, depositories of modern and scientific knowledge that, according to the extensionists, cannot understand due to their profound ignorance. In this way, they make the peasantry feel that their ways of life are of no use and that they must abandon them for a supposed common good. Freire shares some examples and conversations held with extensionists in *On cultural action* (1972), a compilation of texts written in this Chilean period, when he worked at the Institute of Training and Research into Agrarian Reform.

Extensionism and cultural invasion are ever present in the educational system – in educational practice, and particularly when working with children. There are various forms of cultural invasion that go unnoticed, such as the imposition of the word on any other means of communication, the control of emotions from a Eurocentric perspective, the establishment of mechanistic routines or the organization of ways of playing.

When working with children, it is especially important to recognize that they arrive with diverse knowledge, feelings and actions, even if they cannot verbalize them. The word is a basic tool that will develop with the help of the educators as long as time is given to teach it. The ability to intercommunicate using body language, gestures, looks, senses, non-linguistic sounds, objects and space must be facilitated. For example, artistic installations can mediate new forms of intercommunication and perception of the world at an early age (Ramos, 2021) by interacting with the installation elements in the space. Various artistic creations can be used that have elements the children can handle without risk (depending on their age and their physical and psychomotor abilities), such as flour, cardboard, ribbons, pieces of wood, etc., which are placed artistically in a space so that the children can explore and interact with the work through mutual help, to overcome fears, dare to interact in new ways and perceive the world with greater diversity. First, the material used in the artistic installation is presented to the children so that they can manipulate it by themselves. In the next session, the installation is prepared; this can be created on the floor by combining the materials in a visually striking way (as abstract art or as non-figurative forms) or creating an imaginative space with tunnels, passageways, cardboard doors or fabric to pass from one side to the other. It does not need to be something sophisticated; it is enough that it is a place of fantastic creation. The children enter and interact with the space, changing it, adding elements or moving them, and the educator helps them to help each other overcome the obstacles that may arise. Subsequently, time is dedicated to sharing the experiences and imagination created, to activate knowledge and perceptions, and relating them to other knowledge that has been previously treated or new knowledge that can be shared. The result of these interactions is a new artistic work, which generates individual, group and collective self-esteem from a diversity of knowledge and playful intercommunication. Hence, the word develops creatively through communication with the whole body and without separating it from emotions.

Understanding that emotions are inseparable from perceptions and reflection-action, and that they are culturally mediated – differing according to origin, age, gender, social class or the place in which one lives – free and self-managed play provides another great tool for generating egalitarian intercommunication from the knowledge of girls and boys, recreating and reconstructing norms as rich forms of intercommunication and understanding of the world that the adult hand should not restrain. However, the fact that the game is free flowing does not mean that the educator must remain inactive during the process, rather they participate by contributing their knowledge and dynamizing the knowledge and actions that arise in the game so that all the children participate throughout the process, generating relationships of autonomy and interdependence.

Although there is no instruction book on how to dynamize the knowledge of children so as not to act invasively or extensionally, the educator can sharpen their senses to take advantage of the opportunities that arise in the children's intercommunications and provide new perceptions or perspectives on the knowledge of the world. At first, it may seem that less is taught but the question is not how much is taught, rather the depth of the knowledge that is woven into the process through intercommunication, dialogue and collective construction.

References

Freire, Paulo (1972). *Sobre la acción cultural*. Santiago de Chile: ICIRA, Government of Chile, The United Nations, FAO.

Freire, Paulo (1984). *¿Extensión o comunicación? La concientización en el medio rural* (13th ed. in Spanish). Mexico DF: Siglo XXI.

Ramos, Pablo (2021). La complejidad: el arte como entrada a las construcciones colectivas (Degree Dissertation). University of the Basque Country. Vitoria-Gasteiz. Retrieved from http://hdl.handle.net/10810/50096.

Ainhoa Ezeiza and Javier Encina

The Culture of Silences

The *culture of silence* must be taken as a transversal concept running through the thoughts and work of Paulo Freire, with ramifications that intersect with other key concepts (*magical consciousness, naïve consciousness, the oppressed* and *banking education*). Considered as a whole, this draws into stark relief a world marked by those who are recognized as legitimate and having legitimacy, with voice and with word, and by those who are recognized as non-legitimate and without legitimacy, without voice and without word. The *culture of silence* speaks of silencing and muting, the effect of an intentional action to make someone silent, which forces the popular classes to remain silent – even when they can or should speak – not to express what they think, feel and do using their reflective consciousness. An intentional action of domination that numbs the consciousness of oppressed people and inhibits any attempt to recognize them as subjects who have the capacity for transformation and emancipation. In this way, alienating dependence dynamics are generated. These create the belief in the so-called *ignorant* – the oppressed and subaltern subjects – who can only escape their misery and overcome their difficulties through the action of the *cults* – the oppressive subjects – who have elite consciousness, the capacity to understand (unlike the *ignorant – uncultured –* whose limited capacity for understanding is recognized), and a culture that is validated as authentic. In the words of Freire (1990, p. 90), 'the culture of silence is born of the relationship between the third world and the metropolis (...) This culture is the result of the structural relationships between the dominated and the dominators.' The *culture of silence* is a question of social class.

The *culture of silence* is sustained by suppressing dialogue, suppressing open, reflective and critical communication, and by imposing the monologue of the ruling classes, typical of *closed dehumanizing societies* (Freire, 1969). It prescribes the rules of *not listening, denying the word* and *only admitting* that which responds to the hegemonic culture, inoculated in the consciousness of the people, who do not necessarily identify with it – it is the practice of manipulation and the search for servitude. The *culture of silence* responds to a political relationship and a structural relationship of power, with which not only the oppressed subject is depoliticized but also those actions aimed at resolving the unjust situations are generated precisely by the structural determinants that are socio-historically conditioned. The *culture of silence* functions as an ideal strategy for preserving the privileges of the ruling classes, and, consequently, its effect translates into inequality, marginalization, domination and oppression. For Freire, the so-called *ignorant* are cultured people who have been condemned to silence, who have been denied the right to speak, who have had their words amputated, who are banished into oblivion, along with their culture and knowledge. Dehumanizing and anti-dialogical practices that end up turning the oppressed subjects of the popular classes into *objects*, who, when they break the culture of silence, discover that 'not only [can] they speak, but also that their critical discourse about the world [is] a way of recognizing it' (1993, p. 37). And when they do, they open themselves to the path of liberation and emancipation.

For Freire, therefore, the *culture of silence* makes it impossible for the *people to speak* and *to speak with their words*; it prevents them *from being presented* (Freire, 1984) as political subjects with critical consciousness and with the capacity for transformative praxis. A people who are denied authenticity and legitimacy.

The *culture of silence*, as pointed out at the beginning, resonates throughout Freire's thought, becoming, if anything, a metaphorical expression, which harmoniously coexists with the tangible expression of the concept. The term and the concept take shape, implicitly, in the development and consolidation of the Freirean approaches, until they are reflected or treated directly in his work; it is part of the essence of his thought. In this sense, *Pedagogy of the Oppressed* (1970) can be taken as the substrate of what would come to be called the *culture of silence*. Following this path, it is addressed implicitly in the essay 'The People Speak Their Word or Literacy in São Tomé and Príncipe'[5], published in a special issue of the *Harvard Educational Review* (1981). It was also later included, along with other essays, in his work *The Importance of Reading and the Process of Liberation* (1984). Freire does not enunciate the term *culture of silence*, but he does announce the deep – structural – meaning of it in his critical speech. This is one more example of his *say not saying* domain. In his essay, he addresses the *culture of silence* by looking at its opposite: 'What is sought is the effective participation of the people as the subject of the country's reconstruction (…) the critical and creative participation of the people in the process of societal reinvention (…) which necessarily requires critical understanding (…) that is generated in the very practice of participating and that must be increased by the practice of thinking about practice' (1984, pp. 128–9). He speaks of literacy that contributes to the people taking 'their history more and more into their own hands, remaking themselves in the making of history' (p. 130); it allows one to combat intransitive consciousness – typical of closed societies – to achieve critical consciousness, with the presence and recognition of the *ignorant*, who are cultured people silenced by the ruling classes. Such scope is reached thanks to the practice of liberation pedagogy.

The *culture of silence* is dealt with directly in *Education, the practice of freedom* (1969), *El mensaje de Paulo Freire. Teoría y práctica de la liberación* (1972), *The Politics of Education. Culture, Power and Liberation* (1990) and *Pedagogy of Hope: Reliving Pedagogy of the Oppressed* (1993).

The constancy of social conquests must not lead one to think that the *culture of silence* has been not just passed over but suppressed. Quite the opposite. For example, its validity is seen in the curriculum (at the different educational levels: early childhood, primary and secondary) as a project focused on creating citizens. However, this project is not allowed the tools necessary to develop critical and emancipatory thinking in order to reflect on and question reality, with its injustices and inequalities; instead, it is used to develop those strategies that the neoliberal subject must possess to fit into the parameters demanded by such a society. The curricular project establishes the cultural contents considered necessary and key to such training; these contents are presented as the only ones possible, as standardized. Consequently, they are recognized as legitimate, indubitable and authentic. Who they are, who speaks and what they speak about … the curriculum are a hegemonic offering that responds to the interests of hegemonic cultures that possess the power structures to legitimize themselves, unlike the minority cultures or non-hegemonic social groups, who have no such structures and, therefore, are reduced to silence, to invisibility (even though they can be or already are present in the classrooms). We currently have a class curriculum that silences social class. The structural relationships between the oppressors (dominators) and the oppressed (dominated) that define the culture of silence, as Freire understood it, are the mechanism for making the latter beings for the first and not beings for themselves, not people with their own knowledge, with their own ways of being in the world, their own experiences, words and praxis.

These are also cultural contents, immune to social problematizing and to the structural determinants that explain such problems and their effects. All those elements affecting boys and girls *are not contained*. They arrive at school with an embodied reality that has no position or place; and to remain in the system, the children have to incorporate hegemonic cultural contents that are reinforced and regulated by textbooks.

One just has to look at the contents of the three cycles in the social sciences area of Primary Education – which are already controversial when talking about a fragmented disciplinary approach – in order to appreciate the reality that is presented and how it is done as well as the uncritical purity and the depoliticized character of these contents, given that the curriculum itself is political in nature. If we look at one of the content blocks, 'Living in society', the title of which suggests thinking in a reflective and critical way, the aspects established include the locality: the City Council and public services; the municipality; popular cultural manifestations of Andalusian culture and its most significant expressions, emphasizing flamenco as a world heritage site (first cycle); the municipalities, territory and municipal population; municipalities: composition, functions and municipal services; factors that alter the population of a territory: birth rate, mortality, emigration and immigration (second cycle); demography; absolute population; population density; the rural exodus; the production sectors: primary, secondary and tertiary. They also include the production of goods and services, consumption and advertising, financial education, money, savings, employability and the entrepreneurial spirit, and the company (third cycle). From this sample, the obvious question arises: where are popular cultures (beyond flamenco), minority ethnicities, the reality of impoverished people, the world of the working class, the rural world (beyond the rural exodus), the realities of countries suffering poverty, the world of childhood and youth, etc? Where are their voices? To speak of the curriculum's cultural contents is to speak of the culture of silence.

Note

5   As recorded in the work of Carreño (2009/2010) and in the *Diccionario Paulo Freire* (Streck, Redin & Zitskoski, 2015). It is in this essay that the culture of silence concept is developed implicitly for the first time.

References

Carreño, Miryam (2009/2010). Teoría y práctica de una educación liberadora: el pensamiento pedagógico de Paulo Freire. *Cuestiones Pedagógicas*, 20, 195–214.

Freire, Paulo (1969). *La educación como práctica de la libertad.* Mexico: Siglo XXI.

Freire, Paulo (1970). *Pedagogía del oprimido*. Uruguay: Editorial Tierra Nueva.

Freire, Paulo (1972). *El mensaje de Paule Freire. Teoría y práctica de la liberación*. Madrid: Marsiega.

Freire, Paulo (1984). *La importancia de leer y el proceso de liberación*. Mexico: Siglo XXI.

Freire, Paulo (1990). *La naturaleza política de la educación. Cultura, poder y liberación*. Barcelona: Paidós/MEC.

Freire, Paulo (1993). *Pedagogía de la esperanza, un reencuentro con la pedagogía del oprimido*. Mexico: Siglo XXI.
Streck, Danilo R., Redin, Euclides & Zitkoski, Jaime J. (Orgs.) (2015). *Diccionario Paulo Freire*. Lime: CEAAL.

Rosa Vázquez Recio

Dialogue

For Freire (1983), walking towards the achievement of a more human and humanizing society necessarily entails the design of liberating educational practices which enable men (and women) to move from a naive consciousness to an awareness-raising process. This transition demands dialogue – the loving and critical encounter between two or more people – where men and women discover their ontological vocation to *be more*, while questioning their relationships with the natural and cultural world, and thus choose actions aimed at transforming and attaining a fairer world rich in the *we*.

It is through horizontal dialogue that people fulfil and discover themselves as beings in relation to other beings, overflowing the self since human interaction is never the solitary development of an innate self, but rather a recreation of self within mutual communication. It also enables people to come out of themselves and improve or perfect their existence, beyond basic empirical needs. This transition, in an effort to open up to the relationship and its realization, is a consequence of the human being's deep nature, thus it fulfils their needs. Within this process, the word assumes the meaning of speaking and making the world, so that the true word is conceived as a social praxis committed to the process of humanization, in which action and reflection are dialectically constituted:

In such radical interaction, if one is sacrificed – even in part – the other immediately suffers. There is no true word that is not the unbreakable connection between action and reflection, therefore a praxis. To speak a true word is to transform the world.

(Freire, 2002a, 70)

Freire raises the loving encounter as a constituent methodological element within the framework of a pedagogy for liberation (1983, 104), as the 'horizontal relationship of A with B. Born of a critical matrix, dialogue creates a critical attitude. It is nourished by love, humility, hope, faith, and trust. Therefore, dialogue, in education for freedom, communicates.'

In contrast, anti-dialogue, common in banking education, involves vertical relationships of A over B. It is loveless, acritical and arrogant. Thus, anti-dialogue does not communicate, but rather issues communiqués.

Although the concept of dialogue, a constituent dimension of Freirean pedagogy, appears throughout his works, it is in four of them where the limits are amplified, and he explains their importance within the creation of educational practices aimed at the reflective, critical and creative integration of the human being into his/her world. In his work *Education, The Practice of Freedom* (1967), it is concisely formulated as part of the method used to promote a pedagogy of communication as a weapon to defeat the acritical love of anti-dialogue. Years later, in *Extension or Communication* (1969), he analyses the concepts of extension and communication, criticizing extension as a cultural invasion based on an anti-dialogical, authoritarian and manipulative attitude which prevents dialogue from emerging as the basis of a truly liberating education. Subsequently, in *Pedagogy of the Oppressed* (1970), he specified the conditions of true dialogue and influence on a problematizing pedagogy, consistent with the utopia of human liberation. In radical opposition to banking education, Freirean dialogue has to start with the search for programmatic content, which cannot be imposed by teachers, but appears as a result of critical and hopeful communication regarding our situation in the world. The challenge is to create knowledge from the dialogical situation; this entails interaction and the division of different worlds, while sharing the dream and hope of laying the foundations of the *viable unknown* in order to expand our *being more*. Finally, in *Pedagogy of Autonomy* (1996), he returns to the importance of the dialogical stance and the practice of dialogue in a humanizing education, as well as the importance of education embodied by example. 'Vouching openness to others and embracing the curious availability to life and its challenges are fundamental qualities or virtues for educational practice.' This openness can only be embodied through a critical and creative dialogue regarding specific human existence.

As a dialogical educational practice, we will look at a particular experience, the El Puche Community Table, which started in 2008 in a socially underprivileged neighbourhood of the city of Almería. The participants in this community-based organizational structure were representatives of social entities, professionals from different public spheres and neighbourhood residents. The following objectives were set for the project (among others): promoting encounter spaces for social cohesion; enabling coordinated actions involving social entities, public resources, neighbours from the area and public administrations; and encouraging the engagement of neighbours in the urban and social transformation of the area. Prior to its creation, the promoters consulted several actors and residents in the area. Freire considered 'one of the fundamental tasks of a progressive educator, who is sensitive to reading and rereading the group, is to stimulate the group and encourage new understanding of the context' (2004, 18). In the initial encounters – grounded in humility, acknowledging conflict as an intrinsic circumstance of human existence, respecting the other as a legitimate other, and the expectation of learning how to build new horizons – the loving dialogue enabled the participants to identify (during weekly meetings and daily encounters with neighbours) the interests and needs of each group member. These included organizing an awareness-raising campaign to promote the cleaning of some neighbourhood areas, the refurbishment of the sports facilities for children and teenagers to use and organizing cultural events for the whole neighbourhood. It also served to report unfair and oppressive situations inside and outside the neighbourhood and to prepare educational actions which would allow each member, and the group as a whole, to *be more*. The issues to be discussed emerged from the different actors involved in the Community Table, and all were related to their material realities and dreams. This enabled new voices to be incorporated into the dialogue (neighbours, educational centres and professionals from different social spheres); it also amplified their influence and recognition in the geographical space and beyond. The group tried to avoid one of the typical misunderstandings present in a naively conceived humanism, which 'often overlooks the concrete, existential, present situation of real people' (Freire, 2002b, 76).

Within this process, reflection was linked to action, and the first actions, the viable unknowns, were created by the group: an awareness-raising campaign to improve the cleaning of the neighbourhood, the *Pucheando* Cultural Week, the building of Garlochí Park, the creation of the *Tres Culturas de El Puche* Youth Association, the refurbishment of the sports facilities, and the social and educational programme to recover *El Ingenio*. As a consequence of these actions, the neighbours questioned their relationship with the world: What is happening? Why is it happening? Who is benefitting from it? Who is being harmed by it? What can we do to change the situation? Human existence, according to Freire (2002a, 71), 'cannot be silent, nor can it be nourished by false words – only by true words, with which people transform the world. To exist as a human is to name the world, to change it. Once named, the world in turn reappears to the namers as a problem, which requires of them a new naming.' All this favoured the transition from a naive-transitive consciousness, characterized by 'simplistically interpreting problems, underestimating ordinary people [...], the fragility of arguments, and practice that does not come from dialogue, but controversy' (Freire, 1983, 54) towards a critical consciousness, based on a 'dialogical and active education that takes on social and political responsibility and is characterised by deeply interpreting problems' (Freire, 1983, 55) and by a search for collective solutions.

The El Puche Community Table is still in existence, with new actors, new projects, new conflicts, but with the same hope of transforming the unfair situations that occur in the neighbourhood.

References

Freire, Paulo (1973). *¿Extensión o comunicación? La concientización en el medio rural*. Madrid: Siglo XXI.

Freire, Paulo (1983). *La educación como práctica de la libertad* (5th ed.). Madrid: Siglo XXI.

Freire, Paulo (1992). *Pedagogía de la esperanza. Un reencuentro con la pedagogía del oprimido* (2nd ed.). Madrid: Siglo XXI.

Freire, Paulo (2002a). *Pedagogía del oprimido* (16th ed.). Madrid: Siglo XXI.

Freire, Paulo (2002b). *Educación y cambio* (5th ed.). Buenos Aires: Ediciones Búsqueda.

Freire, Paulo (2004). *Pedagogía de la autonomía. Saberes necesarios para la práctica educativa*. Sao Paulo: Paz e Terra.

Domingo Mayor Paredes

Hope

Etymologically, the Spanish word for hope *(esperanza)* comes from the Latin *sperantia* and *speres*, which is related to *wait*. The dictionary of the Royal Spanish Academy (2021) relates all these terms, as well as the word *expectation*. Hope, according to RAE, is a 'state of mind that arises when what is desired is presented as achievable' and expectation is 'the hope of realizing or achieving something' and the 'reasonable possibility of something happening'. On the other hand, waiting *(la espera)* is defined firstly as 'having hope of getting what you want' and as 'staying in a place where you think someone has to go or where it is presumed that something has to happen'. Therefore, in the definition of hope (*esperanza*) and its relationship with waiting (*la espera*), there is a double meaning: one related to capacity or expectations, and another that is more immobile, linked to passive permanence in a certain situation.

Paulo Freire's starting point regarding hope is clearly delimited in his masterpiece, the *Pedagogy of the Oppressed* (1970), the origin of all Freire's thought and a good part of critical pedagogy. Throughout those pages, the author speaks extensively of how oppressors install the thinking of hopelessness in the oppressed through a series of myths, magical thinking and determinism. Hope is not expressly treated in the text (as it will be in later works) but it appears across his discourse. He states, for example, that 'there is only knowledge in invention, in reinvention, in the restless, impatient, permanent search that men carry out in the world, with the world and with others. A search that is also hopeful' (Freire, 2016, p. 62). After including numerous reflections on dialogue and dialogicity, he indicates that dialogue without hope is not possible, and that hope must be shared: 'You cannot think of objectivity without subjectivity. There is not one without the other, and neither can be dichotomized' (p. 38). The hope for change and social transformation appears even in the final words of this book, linked to hope: 'If nothing remains of these pages, we hope that at least something will remain: our trust in the people. Our faith in man and in the creation of a world in which it is less difficult to love' (p. 188).

Hope is a central concept in Freire's work. So much so, that it is impossible for him to conceive of the work of teaching or even of human beings themselves without hope:

Hope that the teacher and students can together learn, teach, worry, produce and equally resist the obstacles that oppose our happiness. In truth, from the point of view of human nature, hope is not something in juxtaposition. Hope forms part of human nature. It would be a contradiction if, incomplete and aware of being incomplete, the human being did not first join, or be predisposed to participate, in a movement of constant search and, second, that the search was without hope.

(Freire, 1997b, p. 70)

Freire himself, twenty-five years after writing *Pedagogy of the Oppressed*, revised these concepts in a work entitled *Pedagogy of Hope: A Reencounter with the Pedagogy of the Oppressed* (2011). Often accused of being *outdated*, *passed over* or *sectarian* because of the changing times and the worldwide triumph of neoliberalism, Freire renewed his emancipatory discourse using the concept of hope. A hope that is clearly defined by action and not by passive waiting:

[O]ne of the tasks of the progressive educator, through serious and correct political analysis, is to discover the possibilities – whatever the obstacles – for hope. [...] This, as an ontological necessity, needs to be anchored in practice. As an ontological necessity, hope needs practice to become concrete history. That is why there is no hope in simply waiting, nor is what is hoped for attained by simply hoping, as this becomes hoping in vain.

(p. 25)

Hope is the key to escaping sectarianism and is in line with critical radicalism. Shortly afterwards he makes clear that 'the struggle for hope is permanent and intensifies, to the extent that it is perceived as not being a solitary struggle' (Freire, 1997a, p. 118); moreover, he relates hope to his concept of *the language of possibility*: 'the new reading of my world also demands a new language, that of possibility open to hope' (p. 81).

Nor is it by chance that in his last work, *Pedagogy of Indignation* (2006), a poem of his appears which again refers to hope, related closely to utopia: 'I will not wait for you merely hoping because my waiting time is a time of work. I will be wary of those who tell me, quietly and cautiously: it is dangerous to do, it is dangerous to speak, it is dangerous to walk' (p. 10). In this work, published posthumously, Freire tells us: 'as a presence in history and in the world, I fight hopefully for the dream, for utopia, for hope, in the perspective of a critical pedagogy. And this is not a frivolous struggle' (pp. 127–8).

For a better understanding of Freire's concept of hope, one would have to go back to Ernst Bloch's *The Principle of Hope* (2007), written between 1938 and 1947, during the philosopher's exile in the United States and reworked when he returned to Germany. Bloch's work already contains the idea, present in Freire, that hope is an ontological need of human beings, that in reality, there is not only presence, but also perceived possibility, hope defined as the ability to invent the future, the possibility of transforming things, from the great political causes to the objects of the discreet everyday world.

With regard to his contemporaries, the influence of liberation theology should be noted and its concept of *liberating hope*, present in the work *Theology of Hope* by Jürgen Moltmann, published in 1964, also the influence of the social struggles of Latin America.

While Paulo Freire was finishing his *Pedagogy of the Oppressed*, in the field of psychology, Rosenthal and Jacobson (1968) published their concept of the *pygmalion effect* or *self-fulfilling prophecy* for the first time, which has so much to do with expectations and, therefore, with hope. The expectations we place on others and on ourselves are always met, whether negatively or positively. From the Freirian perspective of social transformation and emancipation, they are an important instrument used in teaching work, from a critical perspective.

According to Freire, all human activity and all educational work contain hope in one way or another. Without hope, neither life nor education is possible. However, to qualify this a little more, we must explore more deeply his idea of social transformation. Hope in education can simply consist of introducing a whole series of contents to students in an uncritical way. It may also consist of seeking the best way to acquire the maximum amount of knowledge, skills and competencies, or we can hope that people and communities overcome their situations of disadvantage, gaining freedom, critical consciousness and social transformation. It is in this last position that we should situate those practices based on Freire's concept of hope.

Within this tradition we could include a whole series of pedagogical ideas from the early twentieth century (although still valid), such as John Dewey's school democracy, the modern school of Ferrer and Guardia, or the pedagogy of Freinet, among many others. In all of them, students are constantly given the idea that they can reach wherever they wish to go, that they will not be condemned to social exclusion because they come from a context of disadvantage. There are constant confidence and hope, from the moment the school curriculum itself is jointly constructed and a horizontal relationship is formed between the teachers and students. The teacher is nothing more than a guide, a facilitator, someone who is channelling the interests and knowledge of the students, although without losing the perspective of building a better world. The so-called *Democratic Schools* (Apple & Beane, 2005) could also be included as practices of hope.

Likewise, the National System of Youth Orchestras and Choirs of Venezuela[6] is a very significant example. Since 1975, they have been developing a whole series of actions in line with the above. Through music education, providing musical instruments and providing the opportunity to play in orchestras, the programme rescues especially impoverished young people from an environment of drug abuse and crime. Currently, there are more than 120 youth orchestras and 60 children's orchestras, with more than 350,000 young participants. In addition, other lines of work are included such as workshops for making and repairing instruments, programmes for the disabled, a White Hands Choir (composed of deaf children), activities in prisons, etc. The Venezuelan choirs and orchestras are a clear testimony to how it is possible to raise expectations and give hope to disadvantaged groups, and to transform both personally and socially.

Note

6   For more information, see http://elsistema.org.ve.

References

Apple, Michael W. & Beane, James A. (comps.) (2005). *Escuelas democráticas*. Madrid: Morata.

Bloch, Ernst (2007). *El principio de esperanza*. Madrid: Trotta.

Freire, Paulo (1997a). *A la sombra de este árbol*. Barcelona: El Roure.

Freire, Paulo (1997b). *Pedagogía de la autonomía*. Mexico: Siglo XXI.

Freire, Paulo (2006). *Pedagogía de la indignación* (2nd ed.). Madrid: Morata.

Freire, Paulo (2011). *Pedagogía de la esperanza: un reencuentro con la pedagogía del oprimido*. Mexico: Siglo XXI.

Freire, Paulo (2016). *Pedagogía del oprimido* (2nd ed.). Madrid: Siglo XXI.

Moltmann, Jürgen (2006). *Teología de la Esperanza*. Madrid: Sígueme.

Rosenthal, Robert & Jacobson, Lenore (1968). Pygmalion in the classroom. *The Urban Review*, 3(1), 16–20.

Royal Spanish Academy of Language (2021). *Diccionario de la lengua española*. Retrieved from http://dle.rae.es.

Luis Ibáñez Luque

Liberating Education

The *liberating conception of education*, or *problematizing education* as opposed to *banking education*, seeks to know reality in relation to the world and to other beings located in a context and a time. All of this with learning constructed by the people themselves, who participate in the educational act. This stimulates human creativity through respect, questioning, discovery and critical research that starts from the problematization of reality, which, unlike banking education, is not considered immovable, the goal being to transform it. In the words of the author, we can say that knowledge is generated from praxis, that is, from reflecting and acting on reality for its egalitarian and democratic transformation.

There is no hierarchical or authoritarian relationship between the teacher and the student; instead, they are educated together in the same act of knowing through a horizontal process between equals, based on a dialogical relationship where all voices and concerns are heard, valued and incorporated into the educational action. The teacher is no longer the source of the knowledge acquired prior to the educational act and subsequently transmitted to the students, but rather the person who problematizes and guides the learning process. They do not transfer their knowledge but get to know reality together with the students. The conception of students being *empty containers* in which knowledge is deposited is left behind. Therefore, the learner is the subject and not the object of education.

Consequently, this approach does not intend to domesticate, but to offer spaces of freedom from which to generate processes of reflectiveness and creativity in the act of educating, becoming aware of injustices and oppressions, and, thus, awakening critical consciousness for the emancipation and liberation of people from the ruling classes. It is not about educating students to adapt to reality but about developing their critical capacity to transform it.

The concept of *liberating education* first appears in *Pedagogy of the Oppressed* (published in 1970) as an alternative proposal to *banking education*. It is also explicitly present in *Liberating Education* (published in 1973) and *The Political Nature of Education. Culture, Power and Liberation* (published in 1985). In *Education and Change* (published in 1976), no specific reference is made to *liberating education* although the work addresses some constituent elements of it. First, the author reflects on how to achieve the *reflective organization of thought*, specifying three necessary ingredients: a critical, criticalist and dialogic method, the use of reducing and codifying techniques, and the modification of programmatic educational content. Secondly, regarding this latter element, Freire details what contents should be addressed for liberating education in the subsection entitled 'New Programmatic Content'. Finally, he tackles the question of what is *dialogue*, defining it as a horizontal relationship between the subjects, starting with humility, love, hope, faith and mutual trust to generate situations of criticality.

Freire bases this approach on two core ingredients – 'knowing and transforming reality' (Freire, 1990, p. 118). All this coming from the students' analysis of reality in order to fight against their own oppressions.

As a practical example, we will look at an educational situation in which part of the student body belongs to the Gay, Lesbian, Bisexual, Trans or Intersex (LGTBI) group of people. Such an example could be carried out in the Primary, Secondary or University stages of education.

To do this, first of all, certain resources can be used (i.e. videos, readings, images) that allow everyone to analyse and reflect on the prevailing values present in the social and educational reality, through visualization or reading, followed by a reflective debate in the classroom around the discriminations still suffered today by those who belong to or are considered part of the LGTBI community. Likewise, knowing and reflecting on the political and religious influences that have conditioned the sociocultural treatment received by this group throughout history contributes to the problematization of the reality as an exclusive space for those who are oppressed because they do not fit the hegemonic models of living, feeling and navigating sexuality.

After this, it will be possible to contrast these data with the students' experiences based on the following structural questions: What are their impressions and experiences regarding the educational work carried out on the LGTBI collective? Are they included among the contents addressed in education? Is discrimination perpetuated within the educational spheres? What kinds of social discrimination exist? What can education do about it? These questions can also be used to reflect on the subject in class, providing an opportunity to look more deeply at the social and educational needs that exist.

All this forms an axis from which to convey a critical perspective on prevailing sociocultural values that exclusively affect this collective, trying to start from the students' own conceptions and experiences, and guiding the construction of knowledge but in an autonomous way.

In order to follow this horizontal approach to the educational process allowing the act of educating to be shared both by the teachers and the students (who take an active role), the course teachers can propose resources although the students must also have the space and freedom to share materials, ideas and reflections which they consider interesting.

To contribute to the transformative and experiential sense of education, different working groups can be formed to design educational proposals and carry them out in different educational contexts, in both formal (educational centres) and non-formal settings (care homes for the elderly, shelters, associations, etc.). The objective is to make this collective present in the different realities in which the proposals are implemented, while educating in the conscientization of equal rights and opportunities for social transformation.

It is also useful creating spaces in which each group can share their educational proposal. In this way, the groups can be enriched by the ideas of their peers and the students can suggest improvements to the designs. Thus, the learning that emerges in the classroom is enriched by the student contributions and a procedural co-evaluation of the projects can be carried out, taking into account possible erroneous knowledge and discrimination against the LGTBI collective or aspects to be improved relating to educational methodology.

Accordingly, the groups can build and share learning about educational methodology and the LGTBI collective in a cooperative and synergistic way.

The projects must remain horizontal, in terms of the relationships that are generated between the participants, maintaining a dialogical and non-authoritarian approach. Their steps, actions and decisions must be discussed and agreed upon (even voted for), being open to proposals from the students, teachers and workshop participants.

Furthermore, to break with the conception of *empty containers*, it is necessary to start with the interests and learning that the students already possess, as people with knowledge and full of potentialities. These can act as learning possibilities for those participating in the programme: creative skills (drawing, theatre and using technology, etc.), didactic suggestions, and attitudes and reflections on the LGTBI collective.

In this way, education can become a tool for working against the oppression in our society that is still directed against distinct body, gender and desire forms that are not integrated into the prevailing canons, the purpose being to achieve a more just and democratic society.

References

Freire, Paulo (1990). *La naturaleza política de la educación. Cultura, poder y liberación*. Barcelona: Paidós.

Freire, Paulo (2002a). *Pedagogía del oprimido* (16th ed.). Madrid: Siglo XXI.

Freire, Paulo (2002b). *Educación y cambio* (5th ed.). Buenos Aires: Ediciones Búsqueda.

Freire, Paulo, Fiori, Hernani & Fiori, José Luis (1979). *Educación liberadora* (5th ed.). Bilbao: ZERO.

Alejandro Granero Andújar

Literacy (of Adults)

Adult literacy is, essentially, teaching reading *after the deadline has passed*. The existing, normalized, massive, all-encompassing and compulsory education systems teach people to read and write in their early childhood. In these contexts, girls and boys learn to read and write in the first years of their lives, at the same time as they are socialized.

Adult literacy involves *teaching people to read and write who are already socialized*, that is, people who already occupy a certain position in what we call *the society*.

Since the eighteenth century, the history of adult education has included *instruction* initiatives for workers, the popular classes or the disadvantaged population – the Enlightenment years (never better said). However, for a long time, the teaching methods and materials were borrowed from early childhood education.

In the long period of history that elapsed before adult literacy was incorporated into the system of so-called continuing education (in the 1960s), this and other forms of adult teachings were – and continue to be to a large extent – a remedial or compensatory task. It was intended – and is still intended – to give people reading and writing skills and a basic education, people who were not able to *enjoy* a comprehensive education system that was made for them. Therefore, what was normally done – and is still done, even in the most educational and academic environments – was to reproduce children's teaching methods even though the work was carried out with adults, and often with the elderly.

In Brazil in the late 1950s, when Freire began to reflect on education and literacy, he counterposed the mechanical task of teaching, the technique of reading and writing, with the profoundly political work that, whether you like it or not, characterized every educational process, however hidden it may seem to be. For this reason, Freire's literacy methodology places at the centre of the teaching-learning process of literacy not only the social condition of people, but also the situation of conflict and oppression to which they had normally been subjected as a result of their socialization. Hence, through a process of conscientization, they take charge of their reality, learn to *read it* and, from there, to transform it. Freire proposes teaching adults to read and write by choosing *force words* that refer to reality in such a way that education is a tool of liberation that allows them to transform it collectively.

The method has three distinct phases. Briefly, these consist of (1) analysing the context where the teaching-learning process will take place, (2) selecting the most relevant words (generative words) to explain the social situation; normally, these are poverty, inequality or oppression, and (3) designing graphic and alphabetical materials to decompose them syllabically and recombine them into what would be literate work in the strictly mechanical sense. However, as all phases include the direct participation of those involved, the literacy learning process runs parallel and is embedded into the process of studying and understanding the social context in which learning will occur; this, to a large extent, also consists of intervening in the collective reality so as to transform it. On many occasions, especially when the method is applied correctly and honestly, the mere mechanical learning of reading and writing gets somewhat relegated to the background; this does not constitute a failure in any way, but quite the opposite, since it is the task of transformation that maintains and develops the process.

Therefore, Freire's literacy method is a mechanism for promoting social organization based on revindication and, at the same time, a mechanism for mobilizing and educating in a way that defends individual and collective rights, and the right to protest. Furthermore, it holds that literacy is a learning project for liberation, as every educational process must be in essence, which affects both the so-called *learners* and the so-called *educators* equally.

There have been numerous experiences of applying Freire's methodology in the field of adult education. In Spain, along with other sources of inspiration, it has been widely used by unofficial educational bodies, usually in collectives and associations dedicated to popular education. Although the balance can be very uneven, in general, the fact that these processes have been carried out in environments very similar to school has detracted from their qualities. The peak period in Spain was in the 1970s and 1980s when the more regulated educational system did not offer adult literacy in a generalized and integrated way. This led to the intervention of the civil society groups mentioned above. As the design of all the educational subsystems was completed and transformed, literacy simply became the mechanical teaching of reading and writing in official public bodies.

Freire's literacy method, however, has the potential of being applied to any field of teaching-learning, which means to any area of collective life. We will give an example that explicitly links to literacy (although not necessarily) by comparing what is now called *Spanish for immigrants* in adult-education centres. This educational practice enclosed in a purely academic theoretical-practical framework turns language learning into a simple mechanical task, essentially no different from that occurring in what we know as *language schools*. When it was wrapped in the term *castellanización*, as happened when it was first introduced in Spain in the 1990s, it was hardly necessary to make explicit the strong ideological and indoctrinal component imprinted on the teaching of this simple mechanical task. However, once the doctrinal burden of *mission* is removed and we take literacy out of the school-academic framework, it would not be difficult to conceive of a *literacy for migration,* where the migrant population, together with the host population, is involved in a deeply political and convivial teaching-learning process, the fundamental objective of which would not be teaching literacy (which would also occur) but transforming the social reality of immigration. The possible generative words? Fear, foreigner, welcome, work, housing, Spanish, home, law … A process of this nature would evidently require much more than schools, no matter how adapted they were to adults. From the moment that immigration laws, such as those imposed by the European Union, condition the entire reality of migration, and everything associated with it, the political character of these processes becomes important.

But the transformative nature of Freire's methodology is not limited to literacy techniques alone. It is no wonder that he subtitled one of his books *Reading the Word, Reading Reality*. We are certainly deeply illiterate in many fields.

Indeed, we can also imagine how different the *environmental education* taught in any educational centre would be if we applied Freire's methodology to hypothetical processes of *ecological literacy*. It is ever more apparent that humanity is increasingly degrading nature at an accelerated pace. Involving populations in teaching-learning processes that act to reduce the ecological footprint and, therefore, inequality between people, involves a markedly political process in which many conflicting interests need to be confronted. Understanding this conflict, the hyper-industrialized context in which it occurs in many countries, and the underlying mercantile and commercial interests, should also facilitate this study based on generative words leading perhaps to an organized population not accepting what things they should and should not consume, etc. That is what most responsible environmental organizations do, in their own way, if only in the field of information dissemination.

The areas where the methodology is applicable are, as we say, innumerable. The underlying approach remains the same: learning to read reality correctly and learning to transform it. Exploring reality, detecting the fundamental terms of its language, the appropriate ones, and learning to use them (on paper and in the field of action) to transform that same reality.

This is the political character of literacy as Freire understands it and, unfortunately, is far from what is usually found in regulated educational centres, where literacy simply means *teaching to read after the deadline has passed*, with the implicit ideological baggage that this technical neutrality entails.

References

Freire, Paulo (1990). *La naturaleza política de la educación. Cultura, poder y liberación* (especially Chapters 2, 3, 6 and 8.) Barcelona: Paidós/MEC.
Freire, Paulo & Macedo, Donaldo (1989). *Alfabetización. Lectura de la palabra y lectura de la realidad.* Barcelona: Paidós/MEC.

Ricardo García Pérez

Magical Consciousness

Consciousness, the way in which the human being captures, thinks about and interacts with the reality occurring in their context, has three states, according to Freire: magical, naïve and critical. The vision and interpretation that the human being has of the world and of themselves will depend on the type of consciousness they possess.

Magical consciousness, which Freire also called intransitive (*Brazilian Education and Actuality*, 1959) and semi-intransitive (*Education, the Practice of Freedom*, 1967; *Cultural Action for Freedom*, 1968; *Extension and Communication*, 1969), means that the citizen focuses on the interests and concerns of their vital sphere, biologically speaking (Freire, 2001); thus, they do not grasp the problems that are beyond it, do not perceive the challenges posed by reality, since the only data captured are those understood by their lived experiences and customs. For this reason, citizens who have this type of consciousness grasp the facts and attribute them to a higher power that escapes their control and their capacity for understanding.

By attributing phenomena to a super-reality or to something existing in the individual themselves, which is not part of objective reality, the human being fails to understand what is happening; their understanding is limited and incomplete, capturing only part of the reality that is presented to them. In this capture process, they fail to objectify or understand the facts and problems they encounter in their daily life, so the capture is magical and superstitious. This situation leads them to a submission of the facts, without looking beyond the reality in which they are submerged, making them docile, closed in on themselves, exhibiting pessimistic behaviour and believing in superstitions. This causes them to throw in the towel, due to the impossibility of combating the situation, defeated by so much information that they cannot control. That is why they conform to their reality, why they accommodate themselves to it in an uncritical and ahistorical way.

Magical consciousness is typical of closed societies, alienated societies that avoid contact with others. They are dependent on the outside, the oppressors and the elites who run them. This consciousness is subdued by the conditions imposed by the higher social classes; the citizen is not allowed to objectively see the events that occur in their life because they have no knowledge beyond that of their own experience. Being a society that is dependent on the authority that directs it, the response from the people is a culture of silence, since it doesn't participate in the matters that concern it. Therefore, the authorities that lead the people have a paternalistic attitude to superstitious explanations of the facts, protecting the people because they consider them incapable of protecting themselves.

Reality is constructed away from the people, the justification being that they do not understand their function in society in the face of the superstitious and insubstantial responses they offer to new events. This generates feelings of guilt and, at the same time, legitimizes their own authority through 'natural, religious and irrational' explanations (Freire, 1978, p. 15). They give these types of answers because their consciousness resides in a traditionalist framework, prefixed in habitual situations in which they know the consequences of their actions. That is why it is not necessary to question the facts, nor to talk about them with other citizens. Consequently, society does not question the habits or values that it has so internalized.

The people are blindfolded, and they cannot protect themselves because the only education they received has been domesticating and banking. This makes individuals docile as they are not taught to question reality, a reality presented in a limited and fragmented way, without any connection between its parts. The human being under these conditions is unable to find an explanation for what is happening because the education system has not incorporated the problems that affect the people, instead addressing contents that are totally alien to the context of the citizens. In this framework, beings are formed who are illiterate in terms of their own life and their own history; the education is not oriented towards them or for them. The attitude of education towards the human being is one of protection; it considers their life impossible to transform because it is subject to determinism. In this way, the individual citizen is also discouraged from having points of connection with others since their situation is not seen as being the same as the rest. That is why, when magical consciousness is promoted, there is neither community, social transformation nor individual transformation.

To move from a state of magical consciousness to a state of naïve consciousness, education plays a fundamental role. While Freire (1970) points out that everyone has some magical consciousness, the important thing is to perceive it and look for solutions to move forward.

Many schools around the world have confronted the challenges of an education that goes beyond the prevailing magical consciousness with respect to the abilities of individuals – for example, repressive educational practices against people who are autistic, schizophrenic or have Down syndrome. These members of society were excluded and segregated because it was thought the only reason for such states was down to their biological or pathological nature, as defined by reality, by magical consciousness. They were outside the experiential framework of what was considered *normality*.

First of all, the very concept of normality has to be questioned, from approximate orientations to critical pedagogy, in order to integrate these groups into educational institutions, where they can receive stimulating programs, individualized and specific attention outside of that planned in ordinary classrooms. Secondly, one has to defend inclusion with programmes aimed at stimulating everyone rather than only being intended for specific groups. This second stage, in which such issues are reoriented, goes on to define *functional diversity*. Here, the emphasis is placed on human diversity, which enriches the world in which we live, producing a change in perspective regarding human reality.

Ordinary classrooms are overcoming magical consciousness through the work of teachers, families and the support of specialized personnel in cases where more focused educational attention is needed; indeed, these cases have priority in the educational response to all students. Measures are adopted that affect the entire educational centre, such as flexible and reduced groups that allow more attention to be given to student diversity, and measures in the classroom, modifying the didactic programmes in terms of the methodological aspects, and the assessment procedures and instruments. The contents are presented through NEAE, the communication channel used by students with specific educational support needs. At the same time, more appropriate techniques are used to internalize the contents, for example, the use of concept maps. Knowledge acquisition is promoted through didactic methodologies that favour the inclusion of people with functional diversity, project-based learning and cooperative learning, all of which are interdisciplinary. This type of learning encourages direct experience, reflection and expression, because all directly manipulated knowledge is internalized by the students, as well as being knowledge that originates from their daily concerns and their own context, thus proving useful outside of school. The most used techniques are reinforcing activities, which improve the students' skills, carrying out activities with different levels of difficulty so that students can develop their abilities and motivations.

All this is possible thanks to the flexible organization of both space and time, of personal and material resources, the active participation of all the students and the help that they give one another through the cooperative practice of peer tutoring.

The aim of these specific measures is for students to develop their cognitive abilities (knowledge), their artistic-motor capacities (know-how) and their affective-social capacities (knowing how to be) – in short, being able to be with one another.

References

Freire, Paulo (1970). *Cambio*. Bogota: América Latina.

Freire, Paulo (1973). *¿Extensión o comunicación? La concientización en el mundo rural*. Madrid: Siglo XXI.

Freire, Paulo (1975). *Acción cultural para la libertad* (2nd ed.). Buenos Aires: Tierra Nueva.

Freire, Paulo (1977). *La educación como práctica de la libertad* (2nd ed.). Madrid: Siglo XXI.

Freire, Paulo (1978). *Pedagogía y acción liberadora*. Bilbao: ZERO.

Freire, Paulo (2001). *Educación y actualidad brasileña*. Mexico: Siglo XXI.

Saray Martín González

Naive Consciousness

Consciousness is the way that a human being captures, thinks about and interacts with the reality occurring in their context, as indicated in the concept of magical consciousness, the first of the three states of consciousness that Freire highlights.

Naive consciousness is the second state of consciousness (Freire, 2001), the human being reaching this when they have abandoned magical consciousness, which occurs when their interests and needs are not reduced to the strictly biological. They do not feel closer to the natural environment but rather expand their fields of interest and ability to capture the facts that occur in reality and respond to situations and questions that they face, dialoguing both with other human beings and with the world before them, becoming, therefore, a historical being.

Naive consciousness would be the primary stage of transitive consciousness (the first classification made by Freire in *Brazilian Education and Actuality*, 1959), entering a second stage on achieving critical consciousness, which would be the third state of which Freire speaks.

The human being with naïve consciousness perceives reality as something static, as with magical consciousness, immutable and disconnected, seeing it in a distorted way by contemplating it parcelled out as a sum of facts, without seeing their connections and interactions, without any relationship between the different parts. That is because a population with this consciousness does not try or discover, does not look deeply into the possible connections the facts may provide. Having such a perception of reality does not lead them to delve into it or into the problems that they face, but rather to interpret them in a simple and superficial way, reaching vain and hasty conclusions, based on their own lived experiences, not the experiences of those who experiment or deliberately attend to curiosity (Freire, 1978, p. 59). They do not look for the root causes underlying the facts, nor which of them are authentic. They believe that they know everything, based on their beliefs, because they underestimate research, valuing lived experiences more, so there is a strong emotional rather than critical content, which can lead to fanaticism or sectarianism (Freire, 1970). They present weak arguments in their explanations and discussions, the objective not being to clarify the facts nor to seek the truth, but rather to win the argument. Therefore, they are not a subject that seeks to know.

Naïve consciousness is present in a transitioning society, one moving from a closed society (alienated, oppressed, dependent, object) to an open society (decolonized, independent, subject), due in large part to economic and industrial development – a society in which there is desire for change, where there is a certain dissatisfaction with the *status quo*, but which values superiors and undervalues the simple human being (Freire, 1978). There is a certain distrust of everything new, the past is judged as something better when transferring its responsibility and authority, since the position of the people is well-off and gregarious, tending towards conformism (Freire, 1970, 2001).

There are certain inequalities and injustices. Faced with these, the elite reacts with assistencialism, wanting to give solutions that remain on the theoretical plane; in addition, repressive powers and repressive media continue to exist. The population has some degree of democratic participation, but only in unimportant matters, not transcendental ones. This is because the people are still oppressed by the upper classes, since their objective is for the human being to continue seeing the world through a naïve consciousness, maintaining the view of reality from the oppressor's angle. While this does not prevent collective actions from being carried out, the population responds more to immediate and limited interests (Freire, 1978).

Banking education is responsible for perpetuating naïve consciousness through the memorization of contents that are disconnected from reality. Neither this, nor the destiny imposed, belongs to the citizen, nor does it come from the people's own needs because the project presented is not planned with or for the citizens. It is an education that remains peripheral to the problems raised and does not challenge the consciousness of the human being. Even though education systems are modernized and reformed, the process continues to alienate people; new educational centres are created that are closed to the external reality. An education focused on promoting self-development while forgetting social development (Freire, 1978).

Education is fundamental to moving from a naïve consciousness to a critical consciousness, but it must be an education that has this purpose in mind.

Nowadays, relaxation and *finding oneself* is fashionable. These come from positive psychology that prioritizes *connecting with oneself*, whatever the situation. However, the individual remains subject to naïve consciousness through the deployment of a series of formulas, techniques, exercises and messages that promise connection with oneself as a way of identifying one's needs and finding solutions to vital problems.

Critical pedagogy has shown how positive psychology functions by analysing mindfulness, coaching, self-help, etc. All these movements focus the solution to the individual's problems on himself or herself, perpetuating naïve consciousness. Consequently, the best choice a citizen can make is to learn new attitudes, strategies and capacities (banking education) to increase their resolutive possibilities with the aim of overcoming any difficulty they encounter and feeling their life is free and full, believing that it is in the *self* where the heart of the individual's reality lies. This implies that constantly renewing one's skills and attitudes will allow one to tackle all challenges, whether in the workplace, in the family, socially or educationally. Therefore, the responsibility for consequences lies with the individual, with the student, since they are solely responsible for their actions and are the only ones who can take charge of them through effort, study, competence, competitiveness, concentration, etc.

Critical pedagogy has shown that there is no possibility of finding solutions by *oneself* through formulas that find solutions through relaxation of the mind and body. Positive psychology, like naïve consciousness, reduces vital problems to seeking the solution within *oneself*, inquiring about emotions that are negatively affecting one's state, analysing them, taking them on and finding a solution to overcome that personal state.

Interestingly, positive psychology confuses relaxation techniques with the arrival of that *inner self*, in terms of the supremacy of individualism – the individual comes first and then comes society. This idea results in the society itself having a naïve consciousness that erodes the links with others, with values and with points of reference with which the individual can anchor themselves to the community.

This current of thought reduces vital problems to specific and disconnected facts instead of social relations that involve engagement, loyalty and fidelity to society. Consequently, no situation is the same; this is the reason why the human being has to be in a state of constant renewal because there is an obsolescence to their capacities, attitudes and competencies. All this unlimited demand affects the individual, leading them to feel depressed and socially useless, or to educational frustration – school failure – because everything always has to start from scratch. Different techniques have to be applied for each situation, which supposedly strengthen the individual, prompting their *inner energy* to emerge and encouraging their *volition*. Furthermore, in the search for the true self, the subject's behaviour and attitudes are controlled through self-demand, while depression results from the multiple choices they have to make and the consequences that ensue, since all of this falls on the subject.

In school, these techniques should be limited to techniques that enhance the senses, concentration, etc., disassociating them from the idealist *inner self* so as to reconnect it, deepen the connections between what happens to oneself and the social world, identifying the real problematic material, and promoting interpretations that take on complexity and contradiction, reaching authentic and profound conclusions based on collective experiences, coming from the search for the principle of societal transformability.

The search for the *true self* turns individuals into malleable hollow dolls who are always willing and open to new situations even if they are unjust, what Freire calls having a naïve consciousness.

References

Freire, Paulo (1970). *Cambio*. Bogota: América Latina.

Freire, Paulo (1973). *¿Extensión o comunicación? La concientización en el mundo rural*. Madrid: Siglo XXI.

Freire, Paulo (1975). *Acción cultural para la libertad* (2nd ed.). Buenos Aires: Tierra Nueva.

Freire, Paulo (1977). *La educación como práctica de la libertad* (2nd ed.). Madrid: Siglo XXI.

Freire, Paulo (1978). *Pedagogía y acción liberadora*. Bilbao: ZERO.

Freire, Paulo (2001). *Educación y actualidad brasileña*. Mexico: Siglo XXI.

Freire, Paulo & Illich, Iván (1975). *Diálogo*. Buenos Aires: Ediciones Búsqueda.

Saray Martín González

Oppressed

This is one of the terms – the other is oppressive – with which Freire defines a dialectical relationship of a political nature that characterizes certain social structures and transcends towards the ontological.

The concept, to Freire's way of thinking, traverses several analytical levels: on the one hand, it points to the *dehumanized* constitution of the human being, an ontological affirmation that signals their inconclusion as such, the inability to realize their power and desires, etc. This supposes a 'distortion of the vocation to be more' (Freire, 1988, p. 38), an inability to develop an autonomous life project because of a *situation of oppression*. This dehumanization produces a denial of the desire for freedom, alienation in individuals and the repression of a whole set of elements that constitute the completeness of *that which is human*. On the other hand, it refers to the construction of a situation resulting from a historical process, which places human beings into two opposing categories: the oppressors and the oppressed. Lastly, it describes a type of social relationship and how it can be transformed.

Freire firstly explains the *situation of oppression* as that which generates, like a matrix, the division of human beings into oppressors and oppressed. Such a situation may have an objective dimension, such as 'A exploits B', or it may have a subjective dimension, such as 'A hinders B in the latter's search for affirmation as a person'.

Secondly, Freire indicates that such a situation of oppression can only be maintained as a relationship of power and violence. It is a set of provisions and devices that maintain this power. Freire refers to these as *prescriptions*, that is, imposing the choices of one consciousness onto another, which makes the oppressed follow guidelines that are alien to them, preventing them from making their own choices and their own decisions. 'The oppressed as objects, as "things", deprived of purpose. Instead, their purpose is that prescribed by the oppressors' (Freire, 1988, p. 61). This violence, Freire argues, is a process that passes from one generation of oppressors to another, which forms the general conditions of times to come. There is, therefore, a reproduction dynamic that perpetuates violence.

Thirdly, being immersed in a situation of oppression causes the humans who are oppressed to conform as inauthentic dual beings. This is because, while they are oppressed, they host the oppressors within themselves, what Freire calls their *shadow*, which immediately leads to the first problem – how can the contradiction be resolved that, since being human has been prescribed by the oppressors, to be human beings would be equivalent to being like the oppressors, seeking what they seek and acting as they act? Or put another way, how does one know that the actions to carry out and the horizon to aim towards are those of the oppressed or the oppressors? Freire enunciates this by saying 'to be is to resemble and to resemble is to resemble the oppressor' (Freire, 1988, p. 41). He exemplifies it with a simple example: 'as a specific case, they want Agrarian Reform, not to liberate themselves but to own land, and with this land, to become owners' (Freire, 1988, p. 42). Their *adherence* to the oppressor prevents them from recognizing themselves as oppressed.

Fourthly, recognizing oneself as antagonistic to the oppressor does not mean overcoming the contradiction since the desire to free oneself from the oppressor can become fear of freedom, to the extent that getting rid of the shadow of the oppressor means having to fill the void that remains, a void that would have to be filled with different content, that of their own autonomy.

Fifth, the condition of being oppressed may or may not be discovered. In the process of reflection and action on the world by human beings, there can be a critical insertion – consciousness – the consciousness of the oppressed in the oppressive reality. This starts by understanding the concrete oppressive reality not as a closed world from which one cannot escape but as a reality that only limits. The insertion activates a mechanism of objectification regarding that reality, thus allowing one to act on it. However, 'being almost a mechanism of absorption for those who are in it, the oppressive reality functions as a force that immerses consciousnesses' (Freire, 1988, p. 49); hence, the oppressed may not see the order of oppression and, in their alienation, may reproduce the oppressors' actions: objectifying others, exercising horizontal oppressive violence, devaluing themselves by comparing their values and ideas with those of the oppressors, or irrepressibly craving possession, of having more.

To parry the criticisms of idealism that were made against Freire, it should be noted that the book in which he broadly develops this idea came after that which he expounded in *Education, the Practice of Freedom,* which dealt with the situation in Brazil in the 1960s – a society in transition, a society that had abandoned its closed character (i.e. non-democratic and colonial) and was pursuing an open model. Indeed, if you read the earlier book carefully, one can see that Freire was analysing a concrete historical reality using the same categories he would later use for individuals, the situation of oppression being the colonial situation, the desire for humanity being the desire for democratization. If in *Education, the Practice of Freedom* he proposes that the problem lies with the country, in *Pedagogy of the Oppressed,* he asserts that the problem is with the human beings themselves.

Liberating the oppressed from the condition of oppression, Freire says, can only be achieved through praxis, that is, by seeking knowledge and recognizing that such knowledge is a *vital need* – 'in order to dominate, the oppressor strives to stop the anxiety of the search, the restlessness, the power of creation that characterizes life; oppressive consciousness kills life' (Freire, 1988, p. 60). And, in doing so, one cannot become an oppressor of the oppressors, as this would not end the situation of oppression.

Since the *situation of oppression* dehumanizes all human beings, the oppressed and the oppressors equally, Freire considers that 'the great humanistic and historical task of the oppressed is to liberate themselves and also liberate the oppressors' (Freire, 1988, p. 39). To do so, the concrete, current situation of oppression must firstly be transformed. This step naturally supposes that the educational activity incorporates a practice – *mapping and classifying oppression* – through which the students, after studying the subject of oppression as a didactic unit, go out of the classroom and, with a field notebook in hand, try to discover the different forms of oppression in their city or in their village. The direct questions – 'Are you oppressed?' 'By whom?' 'In what way?' 'How can you free yourself?' – could start the notebook at the first level: the level of perception. The activity would contrast the formal reflection of the classroom with the experiential forms in which oppression materializes. These questions would be followed by others aimed at knowing whether their desires and interests are similar to those of their oppressors. This would suppose a second level: consciousness.

Another possible practice would be the *word chain*, which allows us to see where the affective choices of words take us, the ideological semantic fields that they comprise (the world they describe), distinguishing those that reproduce oppression from those that liberate us from it. After collectively performing the chain, all the chosen words and phrases are put on the board and analysed by discussing whether they belong to the oppressor or the oppressed.

Finally, for the self-perception or recognition of our own oppression, something like *Collective Mirror Play* could be used. Since one of the effects of oppression is self-devaluation, a situation could be set up in which two people sit opposite one another, as a figure and an image in the mirror, with the rest of the class as a community chorus, determining which elements expressed by the *humanity* of the two learners are the result of a situation of oppression and which are constitutive of their being. The chorus would never judge but rather inquire into the whys and wherefores.

References

Freire, Paulo (1974). *Concientización* (especially, pp. 63–7). Buenos Aires: Búsqueda.
Freire, Paulo (1988). *Pedagogía del oprimido* (especially Chapter 1, pp. 35–72). Madrid: Siglo XXI.

César de Vicente Hernando

The Paulo Freire Method

This is the name given to the set of procedures, tools, processes and collective dynamics aimed at illiterate people acquiring reading and writing skills. The specificity of this method lies in three fundamental aspects that occur throughout its development: first, that in literacy, the *existential field* of the learners is used, not that of the educators, in terms of both the words of the educational material and the topics discussed, and their determination by situation limits; secondly, in its dialogical character, meaning the encounter between human beings – mediated by the world – which is not exhausted in the I-you relationship; and, thirdly, in the transformative power of the world through a constant cycle of reflection that begins with the speaking of the same, its problematized return to the speaking subjects and the creation of a new speech by them (Freire, 1988, pp. 104–5).

The method was described in a mainly abstract and philosophical way in Chapter 3 of *Pedagogy of the Oppressed*, and then in a practical and technical way in the chapter 'Education and Conscientization' in *Education, the Practice of Freedom*.

The method's exposition involves articulating numerous elements that cannot be covered in a single entry but, in this dictionary, we can establish four phases *grosso modo*. The first deals with the design of the *educational programme*:

> [H]ence, in order to realize this conception of education as a practice of freedom, its dialogue begins, not when the educators-learners meet the learners-educators in a pedagogical situation but before, when they wonder what they are going to dialogue with them about. This concern about the dialogic content is the concern about the programmatic content of education.
>
> (Freire, 1988, p. 111)

Therefore, it is not something given, something imposed on the learners, brought from outside their lives but rather 'the organized, systematized and increasing return to the people of those elements that life gave them in an unstructured way' (Freire, 1988, pp. 111–12). This programme is related to the desires, doubts, hopes and fears of the learners, and always refers to their existential situation. In this first phase, a set of interacting themes that characterize an epoch (time) and a geopolitical field (space) is identified. It is what Freire calls *epochal unity*, that is, 'a set of ideas, conceptions, hopes, doubts, values, and challenges that are in dialectical interaction with their opposites, in search of fullness' (Freire, 1988, p. 123). The concrete representation as well as its contradictory determination constitutes the themes of the epoch. At the end of this phase what is obtained is a set of *basic contradictions* that define the existential, concrete and present situation of the people 'as a problem that, in turn, challenges them, and doing so requires a response, not at the intellectual level, but at the level of action' (Freire, 1988, p. 115). For the purposes of the literacy programme, what you have is the *vocabulary universe* of the groups that you will work with.

In the second phase, thematic and significant research is carried out based on the so-called generative words (in the literacy process) and the generative themes (from the post-literacy process). The idea of the generative word supposes the learners' capture of the relationships that these words uncover and the causal links that exist. According to Freire:

> the generative themes can be located in concentric circles that start from the most general to the most particular. Themes of a universal nature, contained in the broader epochal unit encompassing a whole range of units and subunits, continental, regional, national, etc. diversified among themselves.
>
> (Freire, 1988, p. 126)

All of which involves managing anthropological, sociological and subjective conditions. The dynamics that are produced around the generative words set in motion a complex process of collective meaning that aims to account for the totality of reality. Unlike the reality lived by the learners, this is captured in pieces that do not recognize the constitutive interactions of the same totality. Hence:

> this is an effort that can be realised in the research methodology we propose, as in the problematizing education that we defend. The effort to present individuals with significant dimensions of their reality, the critical analysis of which allows them to recognize how the parts interact.
>
> (Freire, 1988, p. 128)

The result of the educational action is to recognize the dimension of totality that enables learners to grasp and understand reality. More importantly, human beings can transcend situation limits, thereby discovering the *viable unknown*, a liberating horizon. In this research, there is the recognition of a concrete, codified, existential situation (an existential structure fixed as something definitive) that critical analysis proceeds to decode (breaking the constraints and recognizing the structure as something built). In this phase, the selection of the vocabular universe is based on three conditions: (a) the phonetic richness of the words; (b) their phonetic difficulties; and (c) their pragmatic value as a function of their greater commitment to a social, cultural and political reality, etc. For the educational action, it is assumed that the vocabular universe selected allows us to understand the totality of the situation limits in which the individuals live.

In the third phase, existential situations typical of the group are created using representations (graphic, auditory, etc.), with which one works:

> [T]hese are codified situations-problems, which include elements that will be decoded by the groups [...] The debate that occurs around them, as with those that give us the anthropological concept of culture, will lead groups to become aware at the same time as becoming literate [...] These are local situations that open up perspectives and allow us to analyse national and regional issues. The generative words are placed within them, by degrees, according to their phonetic difficulty. A generative word can include the whole situation, or it can refer to one of the elements.
>
> (Freire, 1976, p. 112)

Creating files that help the teaching group members in their work and the design of didactic material (cards, slides, drawings, photographs, etc.) make up the last two phases of the method. For example, the learners are shown an image in which the generative word is graphically represented, and the written word is included. This is discussed in relation to the situations that make up the word. Then, the word is displayed without the image and broken up into syllables to establish phonetic families. When these are produced, a *discovery sheet* is defined that accounts for the productive nature of the procedure; this is then used by the learners to make other combinations. The literacy process has begun.

While illiteracy remains a serious problem in the world (773 million people in 2020, according to UNESCO figures) and it is not difficult to find books and notebooks dedicated to describing the literacy method of this Brazilian pedagogue, the Paulo Freire Method could and should be adopted as a way to promote critical action in schools dealing with issues that undermine coexistence and limit the possibilities of human groups for reasons of ethnic origin. For example, xenophobia, or hatred of foreigners, is a form of segregation, stigmatization and rejection of certain individuals for merely being members of different cultural groups, which, in turn, have been ideologically characterized as inferior, underdeveloped, without humanity and stripped of their rights by other ethnic groups. Considering the various ways of life in our multi-ethnic societies, and the conflicts that are generated in some neighbourhoods and schools, we believe that educator research teams could apply Freire's method to a situation limit that, affecting the whole society and having complex and diverse geopolitical realities, might lead to acts of xenophobia against some members of the school community.

First, research could be conducted on the meanings and sense of the class group's vocabular universe. In it, contradictions would be found that lead to a set of generative words explaining the totality of the xenophobic situation occurring in the classroom. The word selection could be *Spanish*, *sudaca*, *moro*, *equality*, *rights* and *work*. Secondly, the educator research team would add other forms of representation and perception to this vocabular universe, in addition to images, such as the use of touch and music. Thus, we could deconstruct the images into semiotic elements, signs and then form semiotic families. For example, the initial image might be a photograph of a border, with hundreds of people of one ethnicity on one side of the fence and several police officers of another ethnicity on the other, coming into conflict because the former are not allowed to pass. The educational action would develop all the elements of the situation: border, differences, segregation, the use of force, rights, etc. Learners would create semiotic families: other borders, other walls, other examples of segregation, other struggles for human rights, etc. They would be asked to combine signs and situations to create new interpretations of the situations described.

Thirdly, having developed their educational programme as an educational project, the educator research team would apply the same procedure to other subjects (to Music, Physical Education, Mathematics, etc.), expanding and complicating the learners' semiotic universe. In History, one could raise the question of what is a nation, what are sovereign territories, what is imperialism, how does colonialism work? In geography, one could point out the natural riches of certain territories where, nevertheless, the populations are forced to emigrate. In literature and art, one could examine works that have justified certain forms of domination or that have stood up against them – and so on and so on with other subjects. Implementation of the Freire method would be followed by an extension task in the form of *vital experimentation*, a coexistence lasting one week where certain tasks are carried out in the students' homes, applying to their own coexistence what had been investigated within the vocabular and semiotic universe. Once the experience is over, the learners would then present the results to the class, describing the lived experience and dialoguing about everything that occurred.

References

Freire, Paulo (1976). *La educación como práctica de la libertad* (19th ed.). Madrid: Siglo XXI.
Freire, Paulo (1988). *Pedagogía del oprimido* (40th ed.). Madrid: Siglo XXI.

César de Vicente Hernando, Teresa García Gómez and Ricardo García Pérez

Pedagogy of the Question

The pedagogy of the question occurs when educators together with students train themselves in the art of asking questions about the practical problems of their lives, their communities and the knowledge they will build. As we know, with Freire, liberating education comprises acts of cognition, not the exclusive transfer of information, since teaching does not require us to give answers, nor point out knowledge, but rather open the door to one's own life and the process of making known.

The question is a source of amazement, knowledge, research, curiosity, imagination, creativity, desire, scepticism, suspicion, disobedience, inquiry, doubt, etc. There is no advance in knowledge, nor in the learning of a problem since it does not come from a first question or even a more elaborate one. Moreover, not allowing the question and taking everything as decided, transmitted, concluded and irrefutable is epistemologically false as well as being sadly and tremendously dogmatic. As Freire tells us (1997a, p. 26), 'the claim that things are like this because they cannot be otherwise is hatefully fatalistic because it decrees that happiness belongs only to those who have power'.

Questions are essential and vital, and even more so in education; they should not be considered erroneous or valid, nor excessive. They are an irreplaceable device in the teaching and learning process. Freire was clear throughout his thoughts and work. 'The education of the *answer* does not help curiosity at all, which is indispensable for the cognitive process. On the contrary, it signals the mechanical memorization of contents. Only an education of the *question* sharpens, stimulates, and reinforces curiosity' (Freire, 1997b, p. 19). The challenge is to consider how to ignite what Freire considers to be the engine of knowledge – curiosity. This opens up the possibility of problematizing reality, of reflectively knowing ourselves, others and the world; thus, for Freire, this constitutes an *epistemological curiosity*.

Epistemological curiosity will propagate dozens of questions that will be entangled like ivy along the path we walk in life. And Freire decries that soon, day by day in the school culture, these questions will castrate the habitual pedagogy of the answer, the very foundation of *banking education* practices, whose certainties and evidence are revealed as the reapers of curiosity, of amazement and the imagination of those learning.

'I think it's important to look at how there is a relationship between wonder and questioning, between risk and existence. Fundamentally, human existence involves wonder, questioning, and risk' (Freire & Faundez, 2013, p. 60). Freire wishes to show that problematizing practice comes from the dialogical nature of the human being – the person as a finite, unfinished being, who never reaches a total and definitive understanding of the reality in which they live. Throughout time and space, the human being is dialogical and, when wondering about the world, begins to look for others to engage in conversations and seek greater understanding. The question is a way of approaching the world and it can contain more power and value than a hundred answers.

> Education, in general, is an education of answers, rather than an education of questions, the latter being the only creative and apt education for stimulating the human capacity to be amazed, to respond to amazement and to resolve the true essential, existential problems and knowledge by itself.
>
> (Freire & Faundez, 2013, p. 76)

The question also comprises stimulus, autonomy, collaboration, process, questioning, doubt, scepticism, incentive, deconstruction, sabotage and becoming. The question was something already present in classical Greece, with Socrates and his Socratic method (maieutics). Freire also demonstrates the same Socratic philosophy: 'ignorance is the starting point of wisdom' (Freire, 2010, p. 65). Admitting one's own ignorance involves a constant search, a curiosity, not an absolute result that imposes and denies the word, but rather a provisional and questionable knowledge that incites and produces communication, constructs the collective and recognizes others, where antagonistic arguments and contents still remain. The question also appears in the history of pedagogy – in the New School, in active pedagogy and in the Pedagogical Renewal Movements (PRM).

We know that we will not transform the world through education, not in the experience of yesteryear, the book and the word, nor today in a world of computer screens, networks and connected devices working twenty-four hours a day to capture our attention and desire. However, 'the critical educator [...] can show that it is possible to change. And this reinforces the importance of their pedagogical political task' (Freire, 1997b, p. 108). That is why we will continue to enquire, inviting ourselves to ask fundamental questions, urgent, intelligent and absent questions, bringing up places, other relationships, situations, conjunctures, problems, partial findings, differentiated knowledge, co-supervisions, returns, implications; that is why we will participate, make proposals, create initiatives, and dialogue between practices and diverse knowledge. Strengthening the democracy of the group, intensifying trust, mutual help, stoking the desire to learn and know by daring not to know, thus contributing to change, and improving anything that does not work in school, or that causes discomfort for anyone, so as to live better lives.

Education understood as the practice of freedom begins anew every day, this beginning being a regenerative sap that reinvigorates our joy of learning. 'Always start anew, make and rebuild rather than spoil, refuse to bureaucratize the mind, understand and live life as a process, live to become' (Freire, 1997c, p. 121).

In class with students at Granada University more than five years ago, a proposal was made to combine the reading of different texts based on questions, anxieties and one's own preoccupations in relation to the subject. Influenced by Freinet and many other teachers, we started from free, linguistic, dialogical and audiovisual texts. Beginning with a group is difficult, and the students' situation manifested many regrets and difficulties. At first, they conveyed their unease regarding everyday life in the university classroom: among other things, they decried the *technical reproducibility* and dispassionate teaching, the unjustified pace of the classes, the lack of communication between students, the hyper-productivity that bore no fruit, the absence of authorship and meaning, the exclusion of the outside world in the curriculum and the competitive logic. A perverse rationale containing sterile *prosumer* growth and the worst teacher-student casticism prevented the necessary work from taking place – work in which the threads of sensitivity, reflection, listening, conversing, desiring, transforming and evolving the experience of educating ourselves and each other are woven with meaning.

At the start of each class, we began with one or more questions from the students, thus involving them and motivating them to investigate their problems, communities and contexts, and to begin the research path together. The questions themselves triggered further questions in the group which, in turn, involved other questions and answers that provided context, meaning, sense and yet more questions. From these, a process of personal and group inquiry took place. Sometimes, we would explore various research practices inside or outside the classroom. Occasionally, we would go out of the faculty to conduct more experimental academic practices.

The relationships and engagement intensified as more was known about the social environment of their companions, their problems, life histories, experiences and views of the world. The curriculum was split open at the seams, the group democracy (rule of the people) intensified, starting from the dialogues of trust created and the gestures and practices of mutual help that were generated throughout the common work carried out. We all realized that situated knowledge stokes the desire to know, from the moment one dares not to know. Throughout the process there were improvements and changes in learning, communication, relatedness and knowledge. But, above all, there were precise, urgent, previously hidden questions and a burgeoning desire to continue asking them.

References

Freire, Paulo (1997a). *Pedagogía de la Autonomía. Saberes necesarios para la práctica educativa.* Madrid: Siglo XXI.
Freire, Paulo (1997b). *A la sombra de este árbol.* Barcelona: El Roure.
Freire, Paulo (1997c). *La educación en la ciudad.* Mexico: Siglo XXI.
Freire, Paulo (2010). *Cartas a quien pretende enseñar.* Buenos Aires: Siglo XXI.
Freire, Paulo & Faudez, Antonio (2013). *Por una pedagogía de la pregunta. Crítica a una educación basada en respuestas a preguntas inexistentes.* Buenos Aires: Siglo XXI.

Feliciano Castaño Villar

The Politicization of Education

Paulo Freire coined the phrase 'the politicising of education' in his writings from the 1980s when he referred to the political nature of education. He himself explains the moment he used this term:

> In my first book, *Education, the Practice of Freedom*, there is not a single paragraph in which I refer to the politicization of education, not even once. In relation to this progression, there was a second moment, when I had already started my exile in Chile. I began to talk about a political aspect of education or *the* political aspect of education. And a *third moment,* which occurred during my exile in Europe, when I say: 'No, there is no political aspect; education is political.' Education has a politicization, politics has an educability, meaning that there is an indisputably political nature to the educational aspect.
>
> (Freire & Betto, 1988, p. 81)

Although the idea that education has a political quality is present in all his work, he does not use the term itself. A quality that assumes every educational act is a political act and, therefore, the impossibility of its neutrality insofar as all educational practice is always guided by objectives, aims to achieve certain goals, based on a theory, implicit or not, aware of it or not, in relation to the vision of the human being and the world, that guides the educational process, guiding in turn the human being in the world (Freire, 1975). This orientation would explain why educational work is not limited to the time and space in which it occurs, but is part of a more global project, a project of society. Likewise, the objectives that orientate the educational work lead to the choice and organization of the educational contents, methods and techniques used to carry out the action of educating – delimiting what to know cannot be separated from the why or the how. This delimitation always results in directive education, as Freire states, referring to its directionality, which could as well be towards liberation as towards domestication (Freire, 1990). These are the qualities he highlights at the end of the 1980s while in the post of Municipal Secretary of Education in the city of São Paulo following the victory of the Workers' Party (PT) in the municipal elections of November 1988. In his subsequent works, he describes these qualities as democratic or authoritarian (Freire, 1993).

It is this directivity that does not allow education to be neutral, nor, therefore, the action of the educator. A neutrality that is much proclaimed and defended either in ignorance or to hide the choice of one's own directionality. Therefore, the pedagogical discussion would not be about how to achieve neutrality in education but on finding out and analysing what the policy is, whom it favours, and against what or whom the educating action is directed. Freire (2005a) points out that education as a political act cannot be thought of as independent of the power that constitutes it, nor regardless of the reality in which it develops, doing so means that the educational action reproduces the dominant ideology and the *status quo*, reducing this action to technical procedures implemented by specialists. In contrast, when it dissociates itself from power, it is possible to 'work on the fundamental role of the school in transforming society' (Freire, 2005b, p. 62).

Knowing that it is impossible for education to be neutral, seeing it as a substantively political practice, means that educators are political, whether they are aware of it or not, and they are engaging in politics when educating (Freire, 2012) – this is when educators have to choose, have to position themselves, and it is their responsibility to be coherent, shortening the distance between educational theory and practice. This requires teachers to look to their *ethicity* (Freire, 1993, p. 74), to assume their dream, their utopia, which is not limited to the classroom space but relates to their ideal of society, to which society they would like to live in, and to which global project of society they want to participate in. Hence, Paulo Freire extends his consideration of educational action to the action of the social worker, the agronomist, the church, etc.

As there are two possible directions that educational action can take, there are two types of educators, acting either through naivety or through conviction – reactionaries and conservatives or progressives – each having different conceptions of what it is to teach, what it is to learn and what it is to know, their objectives differing as much as the methods they employ, the contents they select and how they select them. The former seek to adapt learners to the world, considering the world as something given. The latter seek insertion into a world that is taking place.

The directionality of which Freire speaks, which is chosen in the act of educating, is evident if we consider the *mappa mundi* with which we represent Planet Earth in our schools. Many cartographic representations of the world have been constructed, each designed according to different criteria, depending on their purpose. This influences the projections obtained, with a variety of distortions due to the difficulty of representing a sphere on a flat surface. None of these projections are an accurate representation of the world. One of the most influential was created by Gerardus Mercator in

1569 as a navigational tool to help sailors cross the oceans; for this reason, he chose to enlarge the shape of the poles in order to create straight lines that served as orientation. This criterion distorts both the position and the size of countries and continents; a distortion that is evident if we compare it with the Gall-Peters projection, first created by the Scottish clergyman and astronomer James Gall in 1855, which coincides with the later version designed by Arno Peters (1975).

Mercator's *mappa mundi* depicts Europe as being larger than South America, when the reverse is the case, and Greenland as similar in size to South America, when in reality it is almost nine-times smaller. Alaska appears smaller than Mexico even though the opposite is true, the former USSR looks larger than Africa when really it is a smaller area. India also appears smaller than it actually is, and Europe is in the centre of the map, not the equator, making the Northern Hemisphere appear bigger than it really is.

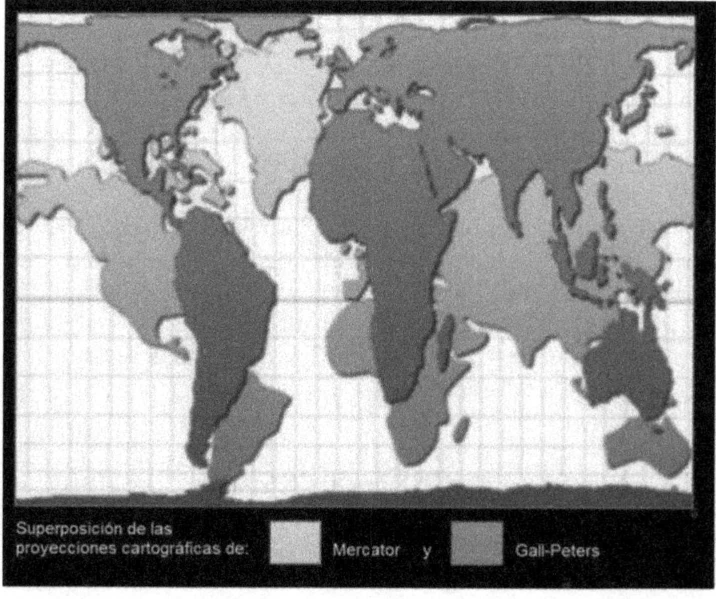

Size has to do with importance and power, as do the position and orientation. Since there is no up or down, the earth is suspended in the universe, and all depends on the position of the observer. It was a decision to represent the North above and the South below, which relates to our conceptions of those who are on top (dominant) and those who are at the bottom (dominated). Other representations, however, placed the East at the top because this is the cardinal point at which the sun rises.

Although the Gall-Peters projection has its own distortions, it does try to represent the different countries in proportion to their territory, so their size representation is more realistic. Other projections have likewise attempted to correct the distortions of the Mercator representation, such as those of Winkel-Tripel (proposed by Oswald Winkel in 1921), Robinson (created by Arthur H. Robinson in 1963) and AuthaGraph (produced by Hajime Narukawa in 1999), the latter is today considered more accurate.

Despite this, ever since European colonial expansion, the Mercator representation has been the world map most used to teach geography in educational centres, in addition to being the one used in the news and by Google Maps, etc.

The colonial, eurocentric and imperialistic vision reflected in Mercator's cartographic representation is evident, a vision that will shape the way we see countries and how reality is represented even though it is not adjusted to their size or position, but rather to political, ideological, cultural and economic decisions. Therefore, according to Freire, when this material is used, the politics of education are clear, namely, who benefits from it and who is harmed, whom it acts in favour of and whom it acts against.

References

Freire, Paulo (1975). *Acción cultural para la libertad* (2nd ed.). Argentina: Tierra Nueva.

Freire, Paulo (1990). *La naturaleza política de la educación. Cultura, poder y liberación*. Barcelona: Paidós/MEC.

Freire, Paulo (1993). *Pedagogía de la esperanza*. Mexico: Siglo XXI.

Freire, Paulo (2005a). *La importancia de leer y el proceso de liberación* (17th ed.). Mexico: Siglo XXI.

Freire, Paulo (2005b). *La educación en la ciudad* (3rd ed.). Mexico: Siglo XXI.

Freire, Paulo (2012). *Cartas a quien pretende enseñar*. Madrid: Biblioteca Nueva, Siglo XXI.

Freire, Paulo & Betto, Frei (1988). *Esa escuela llamada vida*. Buenos Aires: Legasa.

Teresa García Gómez

The Popular Public School

The popular public school was a pedagogical political project carried out by Paulo Freire while he was in charge of the Municipal Secretariat of Education in the city of São Paulo from 1989 to 1991, working within the public education system. The project, marked by its notion of politicizing education, had a substantively democratic directionality. This project involved *changing the face of the school*,[7] an expression used by Freire to refer to institutional change, consisting of turning the school into a space of creativity, where teaching is filled with joy, where children feel comfortable in the surroundings generated in it, making school 'serious, competent, fair, cheerful and curious' (Freire, 2005, p. 49).

The popular public school means respecting the students' way of being, recognizing and considering the culture and how it is experienced as a culture of social class, and not to assess children from the lower classes using the same parameters as those used for children from the middle classes, since these favour the latter through class conditioning. The popular public school transforms its space 'within which the child, whether from the popular class or not, has the conditions to learn and create, to take risks, to enquire, to grow' (Freire,

2005, pp. 49–50). At the same time, it allows the educational community to participate in decision-making, in terms of both school management and the programming carried out in it. It is the right of teachers, students, families, educational agents and the local community to manage their own schools and their own pedagogical projects, which are generated through participatory research. To make participation effective, Freire promoted the School Councils (already existing yet non-functional bodies for enabling the effective and democratic participation of the educational and local community in the school) and the Pedagogical Plenaries, which were meetings held on Saturdays between heads of the Municipal Secretariat of Education from the different *estancias* and the community, to evaluate all the sectors involved through listening, dialogue and discussion.

Therefore, a popular public school is a democratic school, a school of all and for all, and as such must ensure accessibility and permanence. This requires both quantitative changes, referring to the number of facilities and the material condition of the schools, and qualitative changes, referring to the curriculum and the organization, since existing schools exclude children of the common classes because their experience, their culture and their linguistic competence do not coincide with that of the school and the values thereof. This directly influences the rate of school dropout and failure, in contrast with what happens with middle-class children, for whom there is a correspondence between their own culture and that which the school teaches and recognizes. That is why it is wrong to explain school abandonment and failure amongst the lower classes as incidents that occur as a result of the students' own volition or incompetence to learn; rather they encounter multiple obstacles that hinder access to schools and permanence in them, obstacles that are both external and internal to the school, which are structural to them. Therefore, it is the school that must eliminate these obstacles in the educational process and put into effect the right to know, the right to learn and the right to study, just as with children from the favoured classes.

In changing or reformulating the curriculum and its contents, a fundamental aspect for Freire was to avoid it being established top-down by specialists. Instead, the concretion would be carried out by multidisciplinary teams, made up of all the sectors involved in the educational practice: students, teachers, families, the scientific community and the local community. University professors from different subject areas would be part of these teams, thus helping the university to assume its responsibility of training future teachers and to get closer to the school environment, to understand the reality and make it rethink teaching and research.

The contents must take into account the interests and expectations of the popular sectors, consider the *knowledge made of experience* that the students bring to the school, and from there, obtain a more accurate grasp of reality. Contents are taught at the same time as *being taught to think correctly,* which for Freire means connecting the contents with a critical reading of reality, and through them, know the social problems and the reasons why they exist. Therefore, pedagogical practice is not banking pedagogy but rather critical pedagogy – the critical understanding of knowledge through a dialogical relationship and the pedagogy of questioning, significant and relevant to the learner, for which the school 'proposes the construction of collective knowledge, articulating popular, critical and scientific understanding, mediated by experiences of the world' (Freire, 2005, p. 96). Key to this is the educational action of progressive educators who seek to promote knowledge allowing one to perceive that the world shown as given is actually being given, and so can be transformed and reinvented. Likewise, says Freire, the management of time and the organization of the space, materials, methods and techniques used must be consistent with the democratic political option.

For a popular public school project, it is necessary to continually train the educators to promote 'a critical educational practice which fosters curiosity, questioning and intellectual risk-taking' (Freire, 2005, p. 42) – a training based on reflecting on their own practice, confronting the daily problems of their educational activity. This is because the progressive educator seeks unity between theory and practice (praxis) and, being the subject of their practice, realizes a cyclical process of action-reflection-action.

Following Freire, the first step in converting a school into a popular public school (whether in early-childhood, primary or secondary education) would be to create a participatory structure, which might include monthly plenaries and a weekly education committee. In the plenaries, the needs, situations and problems affecting the people as a community are raised, discussed and analysed, and the voices of teachers, families, students, educational agents, social entities, and administration and public resources personnel are listened to. As a result of this debate, a problem-situation is chosen in the plenary session in order to investigate it and transform it. The education committee, comprising representatives from each of the groups, monitors the work agreed in the plenary and addresses specific problems that arise in practice. Both in the plenaries and in the education committee, it will be necessary to look for mechanisms and strategies to express different points of view and to promote real participation in decision-making, thus eliminating any possible conditioning or inhibitions that reside in some groups but are not apparent.

Secondly, the situation-problem agreed upon in the plenary session is investigated in the context of the education centre's location, hence becoming aware of the origin of the problem, its causes and the consequences it has on the lives of the different groups in the community. This means that a research-action is proposed for the educational cycles based on what is known and what needs to be known about the reality being investigated, incorporating into the enquiry the objectives, competencies and curricular contents of the educational cycle or stage. In this way, the teaching-learning work is carried out in an interdisciplinary and globalized way within multidisciplinary teams: teachers, students, families, neighbourhood representatives and cultural associations, social and public bodies and institutions, and other socio-educational agents. The university students and professors also form part of these teams, where the initial and continuing teacher training of both groups is part of a political conscientization project, transforming schools into appropriate community spaces to develop educational projects that problematize the reality. The disciplinary knowledge of the university subjects is linked to this problematization, being a tool for understanding, analysing and intervening in the specific social and educational reality.

Therefore, multidisciplinary teams constitute the training space in which scientific, practical, experiential and existing knowledge from within the community is integrated; this they investigate to plan and carry out actions that transform reality based on the new knowledge acquired, finding the limits present in the transformative action, and studying the possibilities and new actions to resolve them, thus making the knowledge meaningful and relevant.

The teaching time and the school space, which also extend to the exterior space, are organized according to the research being carried out and the aims of each of the phases in which they are developed, using various community or external resources to find the necessary responses to the questions raised.

The research-action carried out will be connected to other problem situations, possibly those already alluded to or dealt with in the plenary session where priority was agreed upon for the current action, thus leading to a cyclical process of the participant research-action.

Finally, evaluation is understood to be part of the whole process, carried out both in the plenary sessions and in the meetings of the education committee, to detect the strengths, difficulties and shortfalls, thus enabling intervention during the research-action to make any necessary correction. The practice itself is evaluated using different procedures: observation, discussion, questionnaires, etc., in short, any tool that provides exhaustive information. The research carried out will also be the subject of a final evaluation that will help decide upon other problematic community situations to investigate in a plenary session.

Another evaluation carried out is that of the students of the different educational stages, to gauge the content they have acquired, and the competencies developed; this will be continuous and formative since the purpose is to enhance learning, not to select or classify the learners. Different techniques will be used: observations, diaries, interviews, exercises, exhibitions, memories, actions, etc., always based on the information you want to collect and the specificity of the group and the people who comprise it.

Note

7   An expression contrary to that of washing the face, used in our context to express just the opposite, a superficial change.

Reference

Freire, Paulo (2005). *La educación en la ciudad* (3rd ed.). Mexico: Siglo XXI.

Teresa García Gómez

Praxis

To unravel the meaning of the term *praxis* in Freirian discourse, it is necessary to relate the concept to Freire's ideological framework. Its philosophical roots are framed in Hegelian dialectical thought and in the Marxist prescription of a practical philosophy, which advocates the transcendence of the interpretive word of reality towards the performative word that changes the world. A philosophy that unites social construction, a word linked to action. If not, it will not be true philosophy[8] nor will it be an authentic word. The idea of praxis cannot be detached from the dialectical discourse in which Paulo Freire positions it, between the concepts of oppression, emancipation and transformation. Freire explains that social reality does not exist by chance but is the product of human action. Nothing exists or is transformed by chance, and if this production of reality turns against society itself, generating a context of injustice, inequality and oppression, it is everyone's historical task to reverse that situation. It is here that the idea and action of transforming reality become synonymous with praxis. Here, at the intersection between the oppressed and oppressor – a dialectical intersection where the first exists because of the second – where the concept emerges, relating to the exercise of liberating emancipation, of becoming aware of reality from a critical perspective, of an emancipation that becomes a search which embodies the concept of praxis:

> Who better than the oppressed are prepared to understand the terrible meaning of an oppressive society? Who will feel the effects of oppression more than they? Who else will understand the need for liberation? Liberation that will not be arrived at by chance, but by the praxis of their search.
>
> (Freire, 1970, p. 40)

These lines are the first time Freire uses the term praxis in *Pedagogy of the Oppressed*, a work written in 1968, in which he contextualizes it in a semantic framework of emancipation. This work is where the bases of the concept are developed, starting from a key idea and defining it very explicitly: praxis is the 'reflection and action of men in the world to transform it. Without it, it is impossible to overcome the oppressor-oppressed contradiction' (Freire, 1970, p. 32). Praxis is reflection and action, it is impossible to reduce it to one or the other, it cannot be translated into mere verbalism or simple activism. It is the way to transform the world and reverse the inequality, injustice and oppression present in our social reality, and for this, it requires the complementary duality of theory and practice, thought and experience, reflection and action. To be authentic, praxis requires a pedagogical exercise that proposes action for real change, that exposes the *true word*. And saying the true word – which is praxis – is to transform the world; to say it is not the privilege of some, but the right of all. For this reason, praxis is described as a collective, collaborative and intercreative exercise: saying the word, referring to the world that has to be transformed, involves a meeting of people for this transformation (Freire, 1970). There is no knowledge if it is not within community: the word needs to be said and heard.

Although *Pedagogy of the Oppressed* establishes the term 'praxis', his previous book, *Education, the Practice of Freedom* (2009), which was the first to be published (1967), already makes an unequivocal reference to the concept as a pedagogical way of change and implicitly alludes to the need to transform the world through praxis. Freire points out that *man digs the well because he needs water*, and this he does because, in that relationship with the world, he places it as an object of knowledge, and through work, sets about a process of transformation (Freire, 2009). In this simple example, the emergence of praxis crystallizes: the human being is a situated being, *to be, he has to be being*, he is subject to the material needs of existence, to social relationships, to vital conditioning factors that involve not only *understanding* but also *action*. Saying that water is necessary is to say knowledge is necessary, to extract the water to drink is to produce not only knowledge but also life; and education provides the path that is constantly remade through praxis to achieve that life.

The concept of praxis runs through many of Paulo Freire's works. Indeed, his work as a whole is a continuous visualization of this idea that goes beyond metaphor as his texts transcend an interpretation of the world and are impregnated with a life of exile, of struggle, of popular educational action in different contexts and nations, and of permanent example. All his work focuses on developing educational practice, characterized as liberating and valuing the exercise of volition, resistance, decision, choice, the role of emotions and feelings, the importance of consciousness and the ethical sense of the human presence in the world, all of which is hopeful and generates hope (Freire, 2001). In Freirian thought, the idea of praxis functions as a recursive political space, a place to which one goes repeatedly to take a pedagogical breath and remember the educational purpose and path: the emancipation of the subject through social transformation. His recursion is noted in the text *Cultural Action for Freedom* (1975), where he points out that human action must assume the necessary proposition of objectives to implement a praxis, or it would be an ignorant action. In his *Pedagogy of Hope* (1993), he alludes to the imagination as a necessary instrument of liberation from oppression. In *Pedagogy of Autonomy* (1997), the text focuses on educational ethics, which he states as being inseparable from praxis. In *Pedagogy: Dialogue and Conflict* (1987), he points out that conscientization is the taking of consciousness to deepen understanding, and that this deepening is generated by praxis. Lastly, in *Four Letters to the Animators of the São Tomé and Príncipe Culture Circles* (2007), the text gathers together educational experiences of literacy in Africa, the place where Antonio Faundez, the Chilean philosopher and collaborator of Freire, remarked that he experienced 'the deepest and most critical period of his pedagogical praxis' (p. 13).

Any pedagogical field, whether in formal or non-formal education, is a propitious space where an authentic reality-transforming praxis can take place. In this regard, interesting experiences can be found in the dynamics of horizontal and expanded education, in which students exercise, as do their teachers, a reciprocal and peer-to-peer education (here, institutional teachers are also involved in the process). A horizontal space where everyone learns from everyone. This is a pertinent method for generating pedagogical reflection and action from the bottom up, moving from banking education to transformative education, where value is given to the learner-educator being actively involved in their own learning, evidencing that the subject plays an essential role in acquiring their own knowledge, and that their participation is necessary for the psychological and social construction of oneself and the collective. An example of this dynamic was experienced at the Antonio Domínguez Ortiz Secondary School, located in the Poligono Sur area of Seville, a difficult context marked by a lack of social inclusion, and where such horizontal learning actions among teachers, students and the community were captured in the documentary *The Expanded School (2009)*.

Another propitiatory exercise of authentic praxis would be to involve students in the decision-making and management of academic life and, by extension, in the community social life of their educational centre. Assuming that the students' involvement directly influences the community's pedagogical evolution reveals that education is a political act. To illustrate this, one can look to the good practice existing in the formal field, such as the educational praxis carried out at the Nuestra Señora de Gracia School of Early Childhood and Primary Education[9] in Malaga, a learning community where assembly management underpins its educational project; this involves all the teachers and students. The students organize the rules that govern the centre through classroom assemblies and collectives, and participate in the student coordination committee. This functions as a representative body with the power to make decisions and suggestions on issues relating to coexistence and the use of spaces (among others). In contrast, in the non-formal education field, we could highlight the educational practice of the Open Cultural Center,[10] a Spanish NGO that provides education to the Polikastro migrant and refugee community and the Nea Kavala refugee camp in northern Greece, where the migrant residents themselves are involved in the day-to-day management. A group of volunteers from the refugee community is part of the team organizing the activities, assuming both management and teaching roles, cooperating with international volunteers and those responsible for coordination. A hallmark of OCC is that it facilitates the empowerment and inclusion of migrants.

Both the actions of horizontal pedagogy and student involvement in an educational centre's management are not experiences that focus on instrumental training but constitute the praxis which emphasizes that speaking the *true word* is to transform the world.

Notes

8   The XI thesis on Feuerbach, enunciated by Karl Marx in 1845, translating in a symbolic and also explicit way the priority and authentic sense that any philosophical action should assume: 'Philosophers have only interpreted the world in different ways, but what really matters is to change it.'
9   For more information, see www.ceipelgracia.com.
10 For more information, see www.ceipelgracia.com openculturalcenter.org

References

Freire, Paulo (1969). *La educación como práctica de la libertad.* Madrid: Siglo XXI.

Freire, Paulo (1970). *Pedagogía del Oprimido.* Madrid: Siglo XXI.

Freire, Paulo (1975). *Acción cultural para la Libertad.* Buenos Aires: Tierra Nueva.

Freire, Paulo (1993). *Pedagogía de la esperanza.* Madrid: Siglo XXI.

Freire, Paulo (1997). *Pedagogía de la autonomía.* Madrid: Siglo XXI.

Freire, Paulo (2001). *Pedagogía de la Indignación.* Madrid: Morata.

Freire, Paulo (2007). *Cuatro cartas a los animadores de los círculos de Cultura de São Tomé e Príncipe.* CD Mexico: La Mano.

Freire, Paulo, Gadotti, Moacir, Guimaraes, Sergio & Hernández, Isabel (1987). *Pedagogía: diálogo y conflicto.* Buenos Aires: Ediciones Cinco.

Zemos98 (Direction) (2009). *La escuela expandida* [Film]. Retrieved from https://www.youtube.com/watch?v=42ZvvuWu0ro.

Carlos Escaño

Reading the Word

As Freire writes in *Cultural Action for Freedom* 'The fundamental theme for the Third World – which involves a difficult but not impossible task for its peoples – is the fight for its right to have a voice, to speak *its* word' (Freire, 1975a, p. 14). In another dimension, it is a human right, to create and recreate the world. For Freire, this dialectic between reading the word and speaking it implies that

> only then can the word of those who are silent, or those who have the mere illusion of speaking, become an authentic word. In conquering the right to speak their word, the right to be themselves, to direct their own destiny, the Third World will create the conditions that do not yet exist, so that those who today try to continue silencing them will instead accept the need to enter into dialogue with them.
>
> (Freire, 1975a, p. 14)

Freire (1987, p. 50) affirmed how the word constitutes a substantial element of the ontological condition of humankind. 'Existence, being human, cannot be mute, silent, or fed with false words, but with true words, words with which the subjects transform the world. To exist as a human being is to speak the world, to change it.' Freire wrote about this comprehension of the word as a force for transforming the world in *Education, the Practice of Freedom* (Freire, 2020).

Fighting for the right to speak, breaking with the *culture of silence* (Freire, 1987) to which men and women have been subjected – this was the theme of another core work, published in 1981, aimed at understanding what the Brazilian educator meant by reading and speaking the word. *The importance of the act of reading: three articles that complement each other* was an opportunity for Freire to teach us that a critical understanding of the act of reading and speaking the world is not limited to merely decoding the written and spoken word or language but is anticipated in and extends to humanity's historical production, apprehending the relationships between the read/spoken text and the experienced context. The reading and speaking of the word, the sentence, must be learnt from the subject's concrete reality, from their *word-world* (Freire, 1989).

According to Freire's famous passage in that book (1989), reading the world precedes reading and speaking the word, meaning that everyone in the literacy process talks critically about their reality during this time. According to Freire's own words (1989, p. 18), 'from the beginning, in democratic and critical practice, reading the world and reading the word are dynamically linked'.

This thesis was taken up by Freire in the company of Donaldo Macedo in the book *Literacy: Reading the Word and the World*, in which, once again, Freire advocates a conception of literacy as a form of cultural policy that should not be confused with the mechanical handling of letters and words, but rather must be conceived '[...] as the relationship between the students and the world, mediated by the transformative practice of this world, which takes place precisely in the environment in which students move' (Freire & Macedo, 2021, p. 6). Language and reality maintain a dynamic relationship. Freire (2005, p. 94) tells us that critically understanding a text (reading) requires us to perceive the relationship between that text and its context. Reading the word is a process that *flows naturally* from reading the particular world (Freire, 2005, p. 99). It is not an exercise in pure automated mechanics in which the subject describes an object represented by letters and words. 'Mechanically memorizing the object's description does not constitute knowledge of the object' (Freire, 2005, p. 101). Nor is it a process in which one expresses one's perception of the object, but the exercise from which the text relates to the world. It is the movement 'from the world to the word and from the word to the world' (p. 105). The reading of the word 'is not only preceded by the reading of the world but by a certain way of writing or rewriting it, that is, of transforming it through our conscious practice' (p. 106). Being able to speak the word means one reads the world differently. Freire (2020) proved that oppressed human beings, who recognize the reality in which they live as the only one that exists, could transform this society ruled by alienated elites, a society in which the simple man is dehumanized and does not have the opportunity to write his own history. The educator heads towards an education utopia stripped of alienated and alienating vestments, promoting change and liberation, in which the man-object becomes the man-subject. To say one's own word is, above all, to recognize oneself as a subject who writes his own history. It is *to participate* in the transformation of the world and with the world.

Freire always believed that, within the historical conditions of society, a wide-ranging sensitization process of the people was urgently needed and indispensable, based on an educational process that would place them in a position where they could self-reflect and problematize their time and space, although the dominant forces would do anything to prevent this critical education from happening. The main task of liberating education is to allow oppressed groups to free themselves from this shadow that crushes them; this is done through the conscientization process (Freire, 2020).

So, learning to speak the word from a critical reading of the world will relate to the type of society we want to build (Freire, 2014). Thus, the exercise of orality is fundamental to critical literacy; this means taking into account the economic, cultural and political relationships existing in each historical moment (Freire & Macedo, 2021).

Speaking the word initiates dialogicity and reveals reality, because from the relationships established through dialogue, the codification of reality and its decoding by dialectical tension appears. Through the horizontality of the discussions, the subject experiences various readings of the world's reality, building their own reading. This power of the dialogical aspect favours politicization, which is participation and action in the real world.

The educational process becomes an important moment for young people and adults to read the world and speak their words with a view to mobilizing and guaranteeing their citizenship. Thus, educational practice, recognized as a political practice, is not enclosed by bureaucratic obstacles and school procedures. All problematized knowledge in this educational context aims to make students aware of their *word-world* (Freire, 1989).

This is one of the main tasks of critical popular education, which aims to insert popular groups in the transition process from common sense knowledge towards a more critical knowledge of the world, involving a different understanding of history and the rejection of any fatalistic or deterministic vision of that lived as the world (Freire, 2014).

In Brazil, after the 1988 Constitution was created, several experiments on critical popular education were implemented in political-pedagogical projects that were concerned with allowing working-class students to read and speak their own words. In 1993, the Center for Research in Education and Culture of São Paulo (CENPEC), with the support of UNICEF, chose fifteen significant experiments from Brazilian municipalities whose educational policies promoted 'the democratization of school management with community participation to strengthen it'.

In general, it can be said that the experiences reported not only questioned the dominant bureaucratic mentality present in the educational systems, but also presented alternatives to their structure and functioning, based on four main principles: democratic management, direct communication with the schools, the autonomy of the school and the permanent evaluation of school assessment, with a view to creating the conditions for a new citizenship to emerge, as a space to organize society, defend rights and attain new ones (Gadotti, 2000). Among these experiments in popular education were those carried out in Porto Alegre (Escola Cidadã) and Belo Horizonte (Escola Plural). These were centred around the aforementioned educational policy based on participatory planning, school autonomy as a strategy to ensure the quality of teaching, building citizenship as a pedagogical practice, creating school councils and organizing the participatory budget and educational content – all this while building the entire educational process from the plurality of existing realities in the teaching networks and valuing the daily school life experienced in and by the entire school community (Gadotti, 2000).

In the circumstances present for the São Paulo and Belo Horizonte experiences, it was not possible for the educators to worry only about the procedures and didactic contents taught to the students, who were oppressed throughout their school career and who arrived again at the school suffering various prejudices and difficulties. Therefore, the problematized knowledge in this context had to relate to the life history of these students, who had to learn to fight for their rights (Freire, 2014). In the context of the educational process, the reading and speaking of the word must be carried out in a dynamic and lively way starting with the students' curiosity, understanding their deep meaning, using texts by different authors or in authorial productions, as objects to be revealed and not memorized mechanically, since this does not constitute knowledge. The movement from the world to the word and from the word to the world must always be present, since words are spoken through our reading of reality (Freire, 1989). The most important thing is that once the conditions in the existential situations of an oppressed person have changed, their word can appear, and they can speak their word. The great question of critical pedagogy would then be – what does the oppressed person say? Popular education incorporated topics such as the dialogue of knowledge, concepts of civil society, cultural policy, the issues of gender and the environment, the reading of the *world of the word*, the valorization of subjectivity, etc., moving away from a purely classist and reproductive reading of education proposed by the military governments of Latin America. With Freire, the public school initiated an agenda of popular education (Gadotti, 2008).

Therefore, the contents selected for the education of popular groups must enable them to critically analyse their concrete reality, overcoming their previous knowledge, which was anchored in pure experience, and directing them towards a more critical, less naïve knowledge. This politicized reading of the world can be realized even if students have not yet read the word, since this process of popular education does not accept the position of political neutrality, but instead respects the students' dreams, frustrations, doubts, fears and desires (Freire, 2014).

References

Freire, Paulo (1975a). *Acción cultural para la libertad* (2nd ed.). Buenos Aires: Tierra Nueva.

Freire, Paulo (1975b). *Sobre la acción cultural*. Santiago de Chile: ICIRA.

Freire, Paulo (1987). *Pedagogía del oprimido*. Rio de Janeiro: Paz e Terra.

Freire, Paulo (1989). *La importancia del acto de leer: en tres artículos que se complementan*. Sao Paulo: Cortez.

Freire, Paulo (2005). *La importancia de leer y el proceso de liberación*. Buenos Aires: Siglo XXI.

Freire, Paulo (2008). *Cartas a quien pretende enseñar*. Buenos Aires: Siglo XXI.

Freire, Paulo (2014). *Política y Educación*. Sao Paulo: Paz e Terra.

Freire, Paulo (2020). *Educación como práctica de la libertad*. Sao Paulo: Paz e Terra.

Freire, Paulo and Macedo, Donaldo (2021). *Alfabetización: lectura del mundo, lectura de la palabra*. Rio de Janeiro: Paz e Terra.

Gadotti, Moacir (2000). Escola cidadã educação pela cidadania. Retrieved from http://acervo.paulofreire.org:8080/xmlui/bitstream/handle/7891/1645/FPF_PTPF_13_009.pdf.

Gadotti, Moacir (2008). *MOVA, por um Brasil alfabetizado*. Sao Paulo: Instituto Paulo Freire.

Daniel Teixeira Maldonado, Felipe Quintão de Almeida and Alberto Moreno Doña

Reading the World

Reading the world is a way of articulating and producing words, of rebelling against the material, relational and symbolic order of the imposed world. Reading the world is to speak the unsaid and veiled, to listen to the silenced, to rethink and write that of the humiliated person, and consequently to make the world. It is a knowledge made of critical experience on a continuous dialectical path of action-reflection-action.

Throughout his life, Paulo Freire carried out a momentous epistemic and pedagogical exercise, woven from the indignation of the theorist and the generosity of the educator. The pedagogy of this teacher from Recife is inextricably historical and anthropological, the world and life are strongly united in his thought. People's lives, especially those who suffer the most, cannot be separated from the world we inhabit. And with Freire, the celebrated dogma of the *end of history* disintegrates by itself, for in the time and space of history, the three spheres – *the world*, *us* and *otherness* – form the same instance. Education is part of that time and space of history and indeed we know that 'no one educates anyone anymore, just as no one educates himself, men [human beings] are educated in communion and the world is the mediator' (Freire, 1970, p. 92).

The world is the mediator, the social, contextual, relational, socio-historical and cultural intermediary. One knows oneself, educates oneself, lives one's life and examines oneself in the world, accepting the world as a mediator, as a pedagogical place. In *Pedagogy of the Oppressed* (1970), Freire points out the core of his argument and programme. The subject is introduced to an evolutionary process of places and develops a series of interactions with other beings and with the world. Modifying, creating, disobeying and responding to the issues of daily life mean mobilizing society, culture and, today, even weaving in a broken eco-social planet. In the world, there are paths that open up experience to other ways of living and conceiving existence, to different social ties between people. Problematization in the educational process will entail the reflective nature of liberating pedagogy, involving a 'discovery of reality from the emergence of consciousnesses, which results in its critical insertion into reality. The more learners become problematized as beings in the world and with the world, the more they will feel challenged' (Freire, 1970, p. 94). To enter critically into reality is to acquire a deeper knowledge of its internal logic and power dynamics as well as an understanding of how culture emerges from the interaction of educators and learners. In the same way, understanding reality means interfering with the edges and limits of history, revealing the discontent and causes of oppression, exploitation and domination of human groups. Always seeking the critical transformation of reality translated into a historical, affective, relational, cultural and vital commitment. Decentring ourselves, getting away from egoism/centrism, classism, ethnocentrism, androcentrism, the hegemonic body norm, as well as any form that makes it impossible for the subject to listen, relate, bond and commit to human pain and discomfort, from entering into a relationship.

As Freire (1991) tells us, the reading of the world always precedes the reading of the word, and that reading the former involves continuity in reading the latter. This dynamic movement is one of the central aspects of the literacy process proposed. Hence, the words with which to organize the literacy programme must come from the semantic universe of popular groups, expressing their meaning, their desires, their concerns, their demands, their dreams, contradictions and senses. The importance of the act of reading always involves critical perception, interpretation and 'rewriting' what has been read.

The circularity of the word involves and links all of us in a crucial challenge that questions our local and planetary community. The reading of the world revives the desire to contribute to the search for new solutions from the diversity of conjunctures and contexts, creating understanding and knowledge through dialogue and discussion between the different worlds of daily life, between different worldviews, epistemologies, practices and knowledge. Freirean communicative and hermeneutic circularity has *praxis* as the first moment and theory as the second. The reading of the world appears as the first instance in the process of reasoning and lucidity. It is in the world where human beings begin the path to literacy, making them conscious of being part of a reality, linking us to one another, letting ourselves be critically affected by it.

Freire tells an anecdote of his childhood, 'I learnt to read and write in the earth around my farmhouse, in the shade of the mangoes, with words from my world and not from the larger world of my parents. The floor was my blackboard and the twigs my chalk' (Freire, 1981, p. 3). This was a literacy far from the letters, words and sentences set out in primers, from a deformed and adult-centric veracity; rather, it was a way of being, inhabiting and being close to the *feeling/thinking* of childhood, distanced from the machine-learning of school. At the same time, reading the world always involves a critical understanding of the act of reading. As he would say later, 'Pedagogy of the oppressed was present as a fundamental weapon of literacy – a literacy carried out as a reading of the world and as a reading of the word, as a reading of the context and a reading of the text, as the practice and theory of a dialectical unity' (Freire, 2005, p. 187).

It is from the sub-alternities and contexts of the exploited groups (in Marxian language, from those dominated and oppressed) that counter-hegemonic senses, practices and knowledge emerge, pregnant with dreams and utopias, in a continuous and unfinished reading of the world, whose nature is the plurality of readings that will require an endless process of dialogue, listening, imagination and discussion. Discussion and the different positions regarding a problem or knowledge are essential, and we must learn to put them into practice, especially so that we can enrich democracy, community self-organization, and the people's social and cognitive justice. 'We disagree with each other almost completely for an hour and a half without the need to offend or mistreat each other,' Freire (2005, p. 217) remarks at the end of *Pedagogy of Hope*.

This way of reading is a dialectical process that unites knowledge, transforming the world and ourselves. This reading, this speaking the world, is an action that makes it possible to distance ourselves from practice in order to deepen our knowledge and critically reflect on it, thus transforming it – recreating the word, the world and ourselves in a continuous historical struggle that enables liberation from all domination, harassment and oppression.

Jinotega, Nicaragua, 2003, a group of primary and secondary school teachers decided to start an educational community whose purpose was to read the neighbourhood (the world) in which they lived. They began by asking questions, starting from lived experiences and fragments collected from informal conversations and interviews with neighbours, at school, the store, the radio, the streets, some clippings from ads, local news, small businesses and the Catholic parish, together with representations and views of various local agents. The practice community met on two afternoons each week during the school year. An intense relationship evolved between the eighteen group participants, most of whom were young women, although there were also five or six men and a third of the group had more than ten years of experience. The cooperative work carried out was enriched by meeting with students, leaders of social organizations, international activists and cooperators, as well as interested neighbours, both those living nearby and from the surrounding city. A plurality of worldviews, social and generational positions, heterogeneous practices and sociolinguistic diversities were welcomed. Very controversial issues came up that generated lengthy discussions and led to some tense moments during the process; however, all this contributed to the essential learning of conflict management and serene discussion. Similarly, various meetings were held in less familiar areas and streets, and the social problems of the locality, and more specifically of the neighbourhood, were explored in depth – health and sanitation, educational, historical, economic, ecological and cultural issues, unemployment, infant mortality, *dengue*, burglaries, unplanned pregnancies, sexist violence, irresponsible marijuana consumption, etc. – these contributed to knowing about and deepening understanding of the social relationships and causes of each of the problems and to develop a comprehensive strategy and methodology that included participatory community diagnosis and planning, following in the tradition of Central American popular education. Action strategies were carried out for each of the issues studied and discussed. Amongst those that materialized were: a neighbourhood men's association against gender violence, citizen security brigades, an unemployed association, an alternative leisure programme for young people encompassing several local bodies and international NGOs and several appearances on local radio to break down prejudices and false notions regarding the neighbourhood, its people and its issues. Throughout the work (reading) of the created community, the relationship between knowledge and improving the conditions (transformation) of the neighbourhood and its people entailed a dialectical process. Likewise, standing at a distance from everyday practice allowed people to deepen their knowledge and reflect critically on it, transforming it; it allowed them to observe, repair, discuss and respond to acts and relationships of exploitation, harassment and oppression.

The community of practice engaged in an intensive work process leading to changes in the people themselves, in their knowledge and self-awareness, and in the relationships between people within their own neighbourhood. Today, some of the people from that group are part of a neighbourhood association (that they themselves formed) in which they carry out a series of actions aimed at improving and transforming the day-to-day life of the neighbourhood and the city. It is especially focused on helping women, children and young people. They also have a community radio school that provides an instrument for participation, community cohesion and communication.

Honouring the dialectical and dialogical work of Paulo Freire involves abandoning slogans, set phrases and prospectives. It means being open to the urgent ethical-political, epistemological, methodological and praxiological imagination that comprises his revised *reading of the world* – collaborating, dialoguing and, above all, in the present climate of dark clouds and stridency, listening to ourselves.

References

Freire, Paulo (1970). *Pedagogía del oprimido* (2nd ed.). Buenos Aires: Siglo XXI.

Freire, Paulo (1981). La importancia del acto de leer [PDF file]. Retrieved from https://media.utp.edu.co/referencias-bibliograficas/uploads/referencias/articulo/524-la-importancia-de-leer-freire-docpdf-mh5tB-articulo.pdf.

Freire, Paulo (1991). *La importancia de leer y el proceso de liberación* (2nd ed.). Mexico: Siglo XXI.

Freire, Paulo (2001). *Carta de Paulo Freire aos professores*. Retrieved from https://www.scielo.br/j/ea/a/QvgY7SD7XHW9gb W54RKWHcL/?lang=pt.

Freire, Paulo (2005). *Pedagogía de la esperanza. Un reencuentro con la Pedagogía del oprimido*. Buenos Aires: Siglo XXI.

Freire, Paulo (2010). *Cartas a quien pretende enseñar*. Mexico: Siglo XXI.

Feliciano Castaño Villar

Situation Limits

In his *Pedagogy of the Oppressed*, Freire describes how systems of oppression develop various modes of control and discipline. For the subjects, the weight of domination becomes so overwhelming and powerful that the possibilities of change are invalidated, seen as impossible and fateful. Domination is accepted as an immutable condition. In the popular sectors, there is a situation of paralysis, fatalism and the acceptance of situations of oppression as something natural. The processes of conscientization and the experience of community groups must then be oriented towards dismantling this immutable perception of oppressive conditions, so that people understand the dynamics of exclusion as well as the cultural and political structures that allow them to prevail. The liberating educational action – eminently dialogical – creates conditions of possibility through a critical reading of the world and its logic of domination. The limits (the walls) that block full human development and the generation of social relations based on inequality and injustice are subjected to dismantling operations through active, participatory and collaborative methodologies, critically analysing their structural sources and the actors and institutions that keep them standing.

This critical reading of the world from the experiences and feelings of the oppressed sectors will open them up and build conditions of protagonism and critical consciousness, making it possible to overcome the *situation limits* (the retaining walls that the dominant system uses to preserve its order and control) through collective actions and community organizing.

The educational-conscientizing process values the knowledge and words used by communities to narrate how situation limits manifest in their lives. It also enhances the individual and collective capacities of the participants to generate social and political changes at the local level but from a global perspective (one's own world and the world for all).

The problematization-deconstruction of the limits that prevent people from fully developing (*being more* in Freire's political ontology) enables processes of ideation and participation in transformative projects. Liberating education then manifests itself as a process of politicization (an *awareness* of one's own world and the outside world along with an openness to collective social and political action) that creates the cultural and organizational conditions for collective action and the projection of what Freire called the viable unknown (*los inéditos viables*).

Freire understood situation limits as challenging dimensions that make human beings grow fully, overcoming the barriers that deny the conditions of freedom for the oppressed sectors. Thus, they are not situations of hopelessness or fatalism but profound challenges that need to be faced to become protagonists of history.

Freire (2015, pp. 122 and beyond) affirms the historicity and politicizing of education as it confronts concrete situations, problematizes historical and political processes, and encourages participants to overcome their condition as limited subjects by affirming their existence as a call for freedom.

The process of conscientization historicizes educational acts and challenges the participants to confront the situations that prevent them from deploying their human projects. Hence, they will not be people and communities that are *closed in on themselves* or fatally immobilized by systems of oppression; rather, they will be *open to the world*, a world they will analyse and interpret through discovery – by *pulling the veil off* the deep meaning of these systems' dominating character.

These dynamics of conscientization, and of individuals and communities taking control, are structured by developing liberating thought and transformative practice (reflection-transformative action), which Freire identifies as praxis. Conscious people then come to know the world, its *epochal unity,* and its contradictions are systematized as thematic universes; these generate reflective-dialogical dynamics that set in motion acts of rupture (*limit acts*) that release the human being and allow them to imagine viable unknowns. Freire understands this process as a de-objectification of the human being and an overcoming of their dependent life, enabling them to become a practical historical subject.

Freire writes in *Pedagogy of the Oppressed*:

Being humans in 'situation' find themselves rooted in temporal and spatial conditions that mark them and, in turn, are marked by them. Their tendency is to reflect on their own *situationality,* to the extent that, challenged by it, they act on it. [...] People *are* how they are because they are *in* situation. [...] And they will be so much more when they not only think critically about their *being,* but critically act upon it. This reflection on situationality is equivalent to thinking about one's own existence. Critical thinking allows people to discover themselves in *situation,* so it stops seeming like a thick reality that surrounds them, and becomes something rather cloudy in which (and under which) they find themselves, a dead end that causes them anguish. This they capture as the objective-problematic situation they are in, meaning that there is engagement. They then emerge from this immersion, learning to *insert themselves* into the reality that is being discovered. As a result of the situational conscientization, the *insertion* becomes a greater state than the *emersion.* This is one's own historical consciousness.

(2015, p. 136)

These categories can be seen in the experiences of community-based popular education in Latin America: educational processes arising from concrete oppressive realities, injustices and discrimination that communities identify as problems affecting their human development and as limitations to their life projects. The *situation limits* are identified and systematized through workshops and dialogic circles along with the dynamics of social cartography, and the maps of the actors occupying the key territorial institutions. The territory is transformed into a unit of analysis by integrating all its dimensions – cultural, age, social, economic – and identifying the tensions and conflicts generated by the dominant policies affecting the life of the communities. The community *in situation* becomes the subject of projects that seek to transform the oppressive reality. Conversational dynamics, participatory action-research, workshops to develop capacities that allow local power to be created, alternative collaborative ways of living, the mobilization of knowledge, cultural self-management and alliances with social movements – all of these foster liberating dynamics that range from the micro-territorial to the macro-regional or national. Therefore, their situationality is given new meaning as: (1) a praxis movement generated by transformative projects (to escape their condition of oppression); and (2) a critical consciousness regarding the lived world and the world to be transformed.

Reference

Freire, Paulo (2015). *Pedagogía del Oprimido* (2nd ed.). Mexico City: Siglo XXI.

Jorge Osorio Vargas

Theatre of the Oppressed

This is the name given to a political theatre concept elaborated by the Brazilian theatre director and playwright Augusto Boal (1931–2009), which comes largely from the theses and methodologies proposed by Freire, defining the issues of trying to liberate the oppressed through scenic practice.

The fundamental objective of the Theatre of the Oppressed is to transform people from passive spectators of theatrical performances into active subjects who transform the dramatic scene. It is what Boal calls the conversion of the *spectator* into the *spect-actor*, meaning that, unlike conventional theatre, the spectator 'does not delegate powers to the character, who thinks or acts in their place; on the contrary, they assume the leading role, change the dramatic action, rehearse solutions, debate projects of change – in short, they train themselves for real action' (Boal, 1982, p. 17).

Like Freire, Boal also finds an ontological dimension in theatre that constricts human beings; this is because humans are the only beings capable of *self-observing* the scene in an imaginary mirror, which is conceived as a dramatic or simply expressive situation. It is the subject observing themselves, or others, who becomes the object of observation, allowing them to reflect and investigate variants to their gestures, modes, actions, etc.

As with Freire, in the Theatre of the Oppressed, there is a process of liberation that goes from the body of the *spect-actor* to the theatrical discourse, creating the dramatic conflict. Thus, the conversion of the spectator into an actor goes through the following stages: (a) knowing the body, its limits, its possibilities, its social deformations, etc.; (b) making the body expressive, separating it from the very forms of expression used in everyday life; (c) understanding the language of theatre and its constructive capacity for situations, dialogues, spatio-temporal areas, etc.; and finally (d) using the theatre as a discourse that elaborates and exposes the meaning of a complex idea. For this, a set of exercises are proposed for the *actors and non-actors,* which serve to develop each of the aspects indicated above. This assumes that, from the start, it is the people themselves who possess the means of theatrical production, namely, the ability to build scenic devices capable of defining liberation through concrete practice.

Freire's essay *Theatre of the Oppressed* (1974) contains a theoretical part, in which a critique is made of Aristotle's 'coercive system' and the limits to the liberation of the oppressed by Brecht's epic model, and a practical part, in which exercises for three of the most important techniques used in the Theatre of the Oppressed are explained and proposed: (a) the *statue theatre* (later renamed theatre of the image), whereby the participants in the session construct three images: one ideal, one oppressive and one showing the transition to the ideal, without using words; (b) the *invisible theatre*, the first step to liberating the spectator, which is a way of intervening in everyday life. It is not performed as theatre, but rather as if it were a real situation; and (c) the *forum theatre*, in which a drama is performed and a short piece rehearsed that is clear and precise, with a conflict of oppression that is falsely resolved. The play is shown to the community in the theatre who, encouraged by a person who acts as the mediator (the joker), offers the audience the possibility of resolving the presented conflict in another way by substituting themselves for one of the characters. The play is thus performed again, but now with *new actors*.

Subsequently, Boal developed two more great techniques: the first, the *rainbow of desire*, intended to free the oppressed subject from the introjected shadow of the oppressor (which Boal calls 'cops in the head') and which resorts to a complex device using techniques from forum theatre, theatre of the image and different psychodramatic proposals; and the second, the *legislative theatre*, which – once again through forum theatre techniques – turns the sessions into forms of popular legislation production, whose results can be incorporated as social demands.

As Freire intended with his pedagogy of the oppressed, all of this means that there is a *politicization of the spect-actor*, a recognition of situations of oppression, and learning that the world is transformable.

After Freire's death, Boal wrote a letter, 'Paulo Freire, my last father', in which he stated:

> With the Paulo Freire Method, we learn how to learn. In addition to learning how to read and write, one learns much more: one learns to know and respect otherness, the other, the different. [...] By dialoguing, we all learn; both the teacher and the student benefit because all of us are students and all of us are teachers. I exist because they exist [...] For me to be, they must be. For me to exist, it is necessary that Paulo Freire exists.
>
> (Boal 1997, cited by Baraúna & Motos, 2009, p. 104)

Within the university framework of initial teacher training, the techniques of the Theatre of the Oppressed, and more specifically the Theatre of the Image and the Forum Theatre, can be offered as complementary workshops in subjects where hegemonic pedagogy is questioned and a critical pedagogy proposed. The students go through all the phases of theatrical work: first, they define a situation of oppression that a future teacher might have to face in a school or institute classroom. In the process of dramaturgical creation, a small work is put together (what Boal calls an anti-piece) and its staging is thought about. Secondly, the work is rehearsed by the people who are going to perform it, while the rest of the class performs a series of vocal, physical and gestural warm-up exercises that will allow them – should they wish – to replace some of the characters in order to take the work towards its ending. Finally, the work is performed as many times as changes occur throughout the session. The entire workshop process teaches students to think about and share situations of oppression in the school environment, identify the oppressors, and their forms of domination over the oppressed. It teaches them to exercise the best interpretative expressions so that such situations are sufficiently communicative and meaningful, and to establish a collective arena for reflection and discussion. Learning such techniques in these workshops is not only useful as a tool in initial teacher training but they also give the trainee teachers ways of discussing conflicts that are occurring in the social reality within the school community.

As a methodological strategy, the Forum Theatre allows one:

1. to understand the educational reality from a critical perspective and fashion the tools needed to construct and develop participatory and fair democratic schools. 2. to understand, analyse and value the ethical and political dimensions implicit in educational processes and in the organization and management of educational centres; and 3. to create alternative responses to different unjust and undemocratic educational practices.

(García Gómez & De Vicente Hernando, 2019, p. 448)

References

Baraúna, Tânia & Motos, Tomás (2009). *De Freire a Boal*. Real City: Ñaque.

Boal, Augusto (1982). *Teatro del oprimido*. México: Nueva Imagen. 2 vv.

García Gómez, Teresa & De Vicente Hernando, César (2019). El Teatro-Foro como herramienta didáctica para el cambio educativo. *Educación XX1*, 23(1), 437–58.

César de Vicente Hernando

Utopia

Very rarely is it the case that the exact origin of a term is known, as well as its creator. It is, however, for the concept of *utopia*, which has its origin in the work of the same name, *Utopia*, by Thomas More, first published in 1516. Five hundred years later, it is striking to see the relevance and timeliness of his proposals, which are perfectly in line with Paulo Freire's concept of utopia. Ideas such as pacifism, social justice, the elimination of rulers, the questioning of private property and money, the right to housing, and defending the six-hour workday, pleasure versus pain, supporting the arts, respecting the disabled, eliminating or simplifying laws, freedom of worship, euthanasia and divorce – all these issues appear in More's book. It even contains several express references to education, such as when More writes:

> [Y]ou allow children to be educated so poorly and their customs to be corrupted from an early age, but then you condemn them when they reach manhood, for faults that, in their childhood, were already foreseeable. What else is this other than making them thieves and condemning them afterwards?
>
> (More, 1994, p. 48)

Utopia is defined from its original meaning as a place that does not exist, but that could exist. We would like it to exist as it shows us a possible future, an alternative, a different and more satisfactory world for people to live in.

It is striking how, being one of the most important concepts in Paulo Freire's work, he barely refers to it directly in his main work, the *Pedagogy of the Oppressed* (2016). More than just utopia, Freire prefers to speak openly of revolution in this work. A revolution that is only possible if coherence is constantly sought between ideology and practice: 'there is no revolution with verbalism or with activism, but rather with praxis. This is only possible through reflection and action, which affect the structures that must be transformed' (Freire, 2016, p. 127). Freire proposes that the oppressed can only overcome their situation of oppression if they connect utopia with practice (p. 54). It is not, therefore, a question of creating new ideological doctrines, but of calling into question any doctrine. Freedom is another key idea in constructing a revolutionary utopia:

> [I]n the theory of dialogic action, there is no place for conquering the masses for revolutionary ideals, but for their adherence. Dialogue does not impose, does not manipulate, does not tame, does not sloganize [...] A revolutionary leadership that is committed to the oppressed masses has a commitment to freedom.
>
> (Freire, 2016, p. 71)

It will be in his subsequent commentaries on *Pedagogy of the Oppressed*, published twenty-five years later in his *Pedagogy of Hope*, when Freire fully clarifies his concept of utopia. This connects directly with the ideas of hope and freedom: 'utopia would not be possible if it lacked a taste for freedom, which is part of the vocation of humanization. Nor would it be possible if it lacked hope, without which we do not fight' (Freire, 2011, p. 125). From his radical critical position, he clearly denounces the postmodernity of right-wing ideology, but also that of the left. Postmodernity is 'too special a time; it suppressed social classes, ideologies, left and right, dreams and utopias' (p. 233). If there is no place for utopia, dreams, choice, struggle or hope, there is no education (p. 117).

Only a year later, in his work *Politics and Education* from 1993, Freire introduces a very relevant idea, related to utopia, by stating that a *living utopia* consists of 'no more discrimination, no more rebellion or adaptation, but rather unity in diversity' (Freire, 1997a, p. 36). Unity in diversity means that it is diversity itself that should hold us together. We have equal rights to be different. Diversity, far from being a source of conflict, is seen here as an enriching fact. Later, in *Under the Shade of this Mango Tree,* he clarifies the idea further:

> The different people, who accept unity and cannot do without it in the struggle, must have objectives that go beyond the specific limits of each group. It is necessary to have a bigger dream, a utopia to which all the different people aspire, and for which they are capable of mutual concessions.
>
> (Freire, 1997b, p. 91)

Utopia for Freire is not an unattainable chimera, but instead lies at the opposite end of the often derogatory and deterministic discourse that is the norm for neoliberalism. Far from being something totally impossible, utopia is something that is built from one's own 'methods, processes, teaching techniques, and didactic materials, which must cohere with the objectives, with the political option, with utopia, with the dream that impregnates the pedagogical project' (Freire, 1997a, p. 77). The starting point in the classroom should be the learners' dreams and hopes: 'I work with people. For this reason, despite the ideological discourse that denies dreams and utopias, I *do* work with the dreams and hopes of the learners, which are sometimes timid but oftentimes strong' (Freire, 1997c, p. 138). History is not written, it is not predetermined, rather it is a 'time of possibility' (p. 73). Consequently, tomorrow is conceived as a challenge, a problem. To achieve utopia, therefore, the first step is the problematization of history. In Freire's own words: 'the deproblematization of the future by a mechanistic understanding of history, whether of the right or left, necessarily leads to death or authoritarian denial of dreams, utopia, and hope' (Freire, 1997c, p. 71).

His final work, *Pedagogy of Indignation*, a posthumous compilation, gathers together all his stated ideas, which are clearly committed to ethics, a theme that carries through all his work:

> [O]ur utopia, our healthy madness, is the creation of a world in which power is so based on ethics that, without it, it is destroyed and does not survive. In such a world, the great task of political power is to guarantee freedoms, rights, duties, and justice, and not to support the whims of a few against the weakness of the many [...] Dreaming of this world is not enough for it to come to fruition. To build it, we have to fight tirelessly.
>
> (Freire, 2006, pp. 143–4)

The struggle for utopia, building a better world starting with the school, is perhaps the main legacy that Paulo Freire has left to pedagogy. Utopia is, undoubtedly, the central idea of critical pedagogy, with Freire as one of its main proponents.

The relationship between hope and utopia is so close that all the practices included in the concept of hope can be considered, to a greater or lesser extent, as *utopian* practices, in line with Freire's conceptions. However, utopia contains an important nuance regarding hope, and this is the idea of *dreaming*, the ability to imagine a reality that does not yet exist. In the classroom or in the daily life of an educational centre, when things are achieved that at first seemed impossible, this promotes the *potentialization* and the conviction that reality is transformable.

There are a lot of classroom examples that contain the idea of imagining another possible reality. For example, Freinet's assemblies or work projects suggest an organization where the students themselves imagine, decide and evaluate their own actions. Another example would be the methodology of project work, carried out in an assembly and from a critical perspective. This methodology has often been absorbed into a traditional and conservative approach through efficiency and the most archaic psychologism, being seen as *one more resource* for the classroom. However, there are numerous examples of project work that would fit perfectly with the Freirian tradition. An example of this is the experience developed at CEIP Clara Campoamor in Huércal de Almería, where all the classroom decisions are made together with the students, without ignoring a range of social issues, such as feminism, pacifism, the distribution of wealth, etc.

Regarding the organization of schools, it is worth mentioning the example of the Learning Communities network,[11] which is based on a whole series of prior practices, among which the Accelerated Schools stand out (Levin, 2021). In Learning Community schools, a real transformation occurs, both in the centre itself and in the wider community, which participates in a massive and joint *dream phase*. This phase allows a sharing of personal utopias, near or distant, simple or apparently difficult, to build a joint utopia at the centre level, where the whole community works together to make the concrete dreams come about. In addition, these schools are organized horizontally, comprising the students and families, teachers and other people in the community. Currently, there are many educational centres in Spain (of all levels and stages) that are developing this project, and many more in Latin America.[12] Recently, this approach has begun to be implemented in Portugal.[13]

Notes

11   For more information, see https://comunidadesdeaprendizaje.net/.

12   For more information see https://www.comunidaddeaprendizaje.com.es/.

13   For more information, see https://comunidades-aprendizagem.dge.mec.pt/.

References

Freire, Paulo (1997a). *Política y educación* (2nd ed.). Mexico: Siglo XXI.

Freire, Paulo (1997b). *A la sombra de este árbol*. Barcelona: El Roure.

Freire, Paulo (1997c). *Pedagogía de la autonomía*. Mexico: Siglo XXI.

Freire, Paulo (2006). *Pedagogía de la indignación* (2nd ed.). Madrid: Morata.

Freire, Paulo (2011). *Pedagogía de la esperanza: un reencuentro con la pedagogía del oprimido*. Mexico: Siglo XXI.

Freire, Paulo (2016). *Pedagogía del oprimido* (2nd ed.). Madrid: Siglo XXI.

Levin, Henry M. (2021). *Accelerated schools*. Retrieved from https://www.acceleratedschools.net/.

More, Thomas (1994). *Utopía*. Barcelona: Edicomunicación.

Luis Ibáñez Luque

SELECTED BIBLIOGRAPHY

Books by Paulo Freire

Educação e actualidade brasileira, São Paulo, Cortez/IPF, 2001 [Doctoral thesis, presented in 1959]. There is a Spanish translation: *Educación y actualidad brasileña*, Mexico, Siglo XXI, 2001.

Educação como práctica da liberdade, Río de Janeiro, Paz e Terra, 1967. There is a Spanish translation: *La educación como práctica de la libertad*, Madrid, Siglo XXI, 1998.

Acción cultural para la libertad, Santiago de Chile, ICIRA, 1968.

¿Extensión o comunicación? La concientización en el mundo rural, Santiago de Chile, ICIRA, 1969.

Pedagogy of the oppressed, Nueva York, Herder and Herder, 1970. There is a Spanish translation: *Pedagogía del oprimido*, Madrid, Siglo XXI, 1992.

Cambio, Bogota, Editorial América Latina, 1970.

Freire, Paulo, Fiori, Hernani & Fiori, José Luis: *Educación liberadora*, Bilbao, ZERO, 1973.

Las iglesias, la educación y el proceso de liberación humana en la historia, Buenos Aires, Asociación Editorial La Aura, 1974.

Freire, Paulo & Illich, Ivan: *Diálogo*, Buenos Aires, Búsqueda-Celadec, 1975.

Freire, Paulo & Salazar, Augusto: *¿Qué es y cómo funciona la concientización?*, Lime, CAUSACHUN, 1975.

La desmitificación de la concientización y otros escritos, Bogota, Editorial América Latina, 1975.

Cartas a Guiné-Bissau. Registros de uma experiência em processo Rio de Janeiro, Paz e Terra, 1977. There is a Spanish translation: *Cartas a Guinea-Bissau. Apuntes de una experiencia pedagógica en proceso*, Madrid, Siglo XXI, 1978.

Pedagogía y acción liberadora, Bilbao, ZERO, 1978.

A importância do ato de ler em três artigos que se completam, São Paulo, Cortez/Autores Associados, 1982. There is a Spanish translation: *La importancia del acto de leer y el proceso de liberación*, Mexico, Siglo XXI, 2005.

The politics of education: Culture, power and liberation, Hadley, MA, Bergin & Garvey, 1985. There is a Spanish translation: *La naturaleza política de la educación. Cultura, poder y liberación*, Barcelona, Paidós/MEC, 1990.

Freire, Paulo & Betto, Frei: *Essa escola chamada vida*, São Paulo, Atica, 1985. There is a Spanish translation: *Esa escuela llamada vida*, Buenos Aires, Legasa, 1988.

Freire, Paulo & Faundez, Antonio: *Por uma pedagogia da pregunta*, Rio de Janeiro, Paz e Terra, 1985. There is a Spanish translation: *Por una pedagogía de la pregunta*, Xativa, Valencia, Ediciones del CREC, 2010.

Freire, Paulo & Shor, Ira: *Medo e Ousadia*, Rio de Janeiro, Paz e Terra, 1986. There is a Spanish translation: Miedo y osadía, Buenos Aires, Siglo XXI, 2014.

Freire, Paulo & Macedo, Donaldo: *Literacy: Reading the word and the world*, Hadley, MA, Bergin & Garvey, 1987. There is a Spanish translation: *Alfabetización. Lectura de la palabra y lectura de la realidad*, Barcelona, Paidós/MEC, 1989.

A educação na cidade, Sao Paulo, Cortez, 1991. There is a Spanish translation: *La educación en la ciudad*, Mexico, Siglo XXI, 2005.

Pedagogia da esperança: um reencontro com a pedagogia do oprimido, Río de Janeiro, Paz e Terra, 1992. There is a Spanish translation: *Pedagogía de la esperanza*, Mexico, Siglo XXI, 2009.

Política e educação, São Paulo, Cortez, 1993. There is a Spanish translation: *Política y educación*, Mexico, Siglo XXI, 2001.

Professora sim; lia não: cartas a quem ousa ensinar, São Paulo, Olho D'Água, 1993. There is a Spanish translation: *Cartas a quien pretende enseñar*, Madrid, Biblioteca Nueva, Siglo XXI, 2012.

Cartas a Cristina, São Paulo, Paz e Terra, 1994. There is a Spanish translation: *Cartas a Cristina. Reflexiones sobre mi vida y mi trabajo*, Mexico, Siglo XXI, 2005.

À sombra desta mangueira, São Paulo, Olho D'Água, 1995. There is a Spanish translation: *A la sombra de este árbol*, Barcelona, El Roure, 1997.

Pedagogia da autonomia. Saberes necessários à práctica educativa, São Paulo, Paz e Terra, 1996. There is a Spanish translation: *Pedagogía de la autonomía*, Mexico, Siglo XXI, 2009.

Pedagogia da indignaçao. Cartas pedagógicas e outros escritos, São Paulo, UNESP, 2000. There is a Spanish translation: *Pedagogía de la indignación*, Madrid, Morata, 2001.

El grito manso, Argentina, Siglo XXI, 2003.

Pedagogia da tolerância, São Paulo, UNESP, 2005. There is a Spanish translation: *Pedagogía de la tolerancia*, Buenos Aires, Fondo de Cultura Económica, 2006.

Pedagogia do Compromisso. América Latina e Educaçao Popular, São Paulo, Villa das Letras, 2007. There is a Spanish translation: *Pedagogía del Compromiso. América Latina y Educación Popular*, Barcelona, Hipatia, 2009.

Pedagogia dos sonhos possíveis, São Paulo, UNESP, 2001. There is a Spanish translation in two volumes: *Pedagogía de los sueños posibles*, Buenos Aires, Siglo XXI, 2015 and *El maestro sin recetas*, Buenos Aires, Siglo XXI, 2016.

Books and Chapters about Paulo Freire

Araújo Freire, Ana Mª (2006). *Paulo Freire. Uma história de vida.* Sao Paulo: Villa das Letras Editora.

Blanco, Rogelio (1995). *La pedagogía de Paulo Freire* (3rd ed.). Madrid: Endymion.

Darder, Antonia (2017). *Freire y educación.* Madrid: Morata.

Gadotti, Moacir (1991). *Paulo Freire. Su vida y su obra.* Bogota-Colombia: CODECAL.

Gadotti, Moacir y Torres, Carlos Alberto (Comp.) (2001). *Paulo Freire. Una biobibliografía.* Mexico: Siglo XXI.

García Gómez, Teresa (2015). Editor of *Paulo Freire. Pedagogía liberadora.* Madrid: Los Libros de la Catarata.

Gómez García, Mª Nieves (1982). *Los conceptos educativos en la obra de Paulo Freire.* Madrid: Anaya.

Kohan, Walter (2020). *Paulo Freire más que nunca: una biografía filosófica.* Buenos Aires: CLACSO.

McLaren, Peter (2001). El hombre de la barba gris. In *El Che Guevara, Paulo Freire y la pedagogía de la revolución* (pp. 183–238). Mexico: Siglo XXI.

Monclús, Antonio (1988). *Pedagogía de la contradicción: Paulo Freire.* Barcelona: Anthropos.

Ruiz Olabuénaga, José I., Morales, Pedro y Marroquín, Manuel (1975). *Paulo Freire. Concientización y andragogía*. Argentina: Paidós.

Streck, Danilo R., Redin, Euclides y Zitkoski, Jaime J. (Orgs.) (2015). *Diccionario Paulo Freire*. Lima: CEAAL.

Torres, Carlos Alberto (1978). *La praxis educativa de Paulo Freire*. Mexico: Ediciones Guernika.

Torres, Carlos Alberto (1980). *Paulo Freire. Educación y concientización*. Salamanca: Ediciones Sígueme.

Trilla, Jaume (1993). Educación de adultos. In *Otras educaciones. Animación sociocultural, formación de adultos y ciudad educativa* (pp. 139–75). Barcelona: Anthropos.

INDEX